Book Endorsements

At a time when some sons make money with memoirs that emphasize the warts of prominent fathers, it's good to have a respectful account of a godly dad.

–Marvin Olasky
Editor-in-Chief
World

Dr. Tommy Lea was a man of God and great teacher who impacted to the lives of many students. I am grateful to his son Cliff for sharing the insights and life lessons he learned from his dad. I consider *"Give Me Your Heart"* a must read for every father and son.

–Dr. Ed Young,
Senior Pastor
Second Baptist Church
Houston, Texas

The greatest need in our homes is for our parents to model the lifestyle of Jesus Christ; not just by what they say (exhortation), but by what they live (emulation). Cliff's father, undoubtedly, left an incredible blueprint for his son to follow. This is a great need in the homes of America. Read, be instructed, be encouraged, be blessed, and pass it on.

–Johnny Hunt
Pastor, First Baptist Church, Woodstock, Georgia
President, Southern Baptist Convention

Few bonds can match that of between father and son. Cliff Lea has captured the heart of this often unique and always significant relationship. The counsel his father gave to him is clearly and powerfully recorded in the words of this book. Read them to your blessing. Apply that counsel to your life and you will be enriched.

–Jimmy Draper
Past President
Lifeway Christian Resources

"Give Me Your Heart" is a beautiful book written by Cliff Lea in remembrance of his father, Tommy Lea. I had the wonderful privilege to know and serve with Tommy Lea, who was indeed a man with a heart for God. Tommy Lea was a gifted expositor of God's Word, a faithful pastor, a fine New Testament scholar, and a loyal seminary administrator. But even beyond these things, Tommy Lea was a deeply devoted father and a loving husband. Cliff Lea's work captures the heart of this man whose life influenced so many men and women during his days on the earth. I heartily commend this work to others.

–David S. Dockery
President
Union University

Tommy Lea was a fine teacher in the seminary classroom and in the classroom of life. Cliff has done us all a favor as he allows us to join him at his father's feet for a lifetime of learning.

–Ken Hemphill
National Strategist for Empowering Kingdom Growth, the SBC

"It has been my great privilege in the past to serve as pastor to Dr. Tommy Lea, and to his son Pastor Cliff Lea. During this time, I witnessed first-hand the extraordinary life of Tommy Lea. Cliff's tender heart for God is a direct result of the heart-connection Cliff enjoyed with his father. The insights in this book will enrich the life of any man wanting to powerfully impact the lives of his wife and children."

–Michael D. Dean
Senior Pastor
Travis Avenue Baptist Church
Fort Worth, Texas

"In an unprecedented era of the diminishing role of fatherhood, Cliff Lea, the Senior Pastor of First Baptist Church in Leesburg, Florida, has penned a book that every father serious about his task needs to read. This volume, based on what he learned from his great pastor/theologian father, Dr. Tommy Lea, who gave himself so stupendously to students here at Southwestern Seminary, demonstrates beyond question that Dr. Lea also gave himself unrelentingly to his own son. Do not miss this book."

–Paige Patterson
Southwestern Baptist Theological Seminary
Fort Worth, Texas

I never had the privilege of sitting under Cliff's father's teaching, but I have shared with men who had and they were unanimous in saying that Tommy Lea was one of the great statesmen of the Christian faith. The qualities found in his dad are reflected in the son. The book, *"Give Me Your Heart"* will lift, encourage and bless you as you read it!

–Dr. Charles Roesel
Pastor Emeritus
First Baptist Church of Leesburg, FL

I have been waiting for *Give me Your Heart* since Cliff and I first talked about it. Tommy Lea was my spiritual father, friend, and closest confidant during his brief life. I never made a major decision or resolved an important issue that I did not seek his counsel. To have known him, served on two church staffs with him, and have his influence was a privilege I hold tightly. Cliff Lea has captured in this book the things Tommy inspired all who knew him to become. In addition, the warm reflections of a loving son make each page come to life with spiritual truths, humorous vignettes, and challenges. You will enjoy this book and treasure both the author and his father as you read it.

–Gene Mims
Judson Baptist Church
Nashville, Tn.

*"Cliff reminds some of us of the precious memories of a God-honoring dad who loved us deeply. He also encourages all dads to emulate his father's example for our children."

–Jim Richards
Executive Director
Southern Baptists of Texas Convention

"I have known Cliff Lea many years as a peer in ministry, and friend. He is a spiritual giant who loves God, loves his wife and children, and loves God's people. He and his earthly father, the late Dr. Tommy Lea, were united in life by their Heavenly Father. Reading Cliff's book, *Give Me Your Heart,* reveals why Cliff Lea is all that God has developed him to be, and challenges all men and women to nurture their children through example and leadership."

–Charles Price
Executive Director
San Antonio Baptist Association

"Having worked with Cliff in ministry and having sat with Tommy in the seminary classroom, I can say Cliff has captured the heart and spirit of his father in *"Give Me Your Heart"*. Cliff has mined his father's heart like Tommy had mined the Scriptures for truth. Every father should read this important work and commit himself to raising his children according to these ways."

–Robby Peters
First Baptist Church
Weston, Florida

Give Me Your Heart

Cliff Lea

CrossBooks™
1663 Liberty Drive Suite 300
Bloomington, IN 47403
www.crossbooks.com
Phone: 1-866-879-0502

First published by CrossBooks on.5/22/2009

ISBN: 978-1-6150-7033-6 (sc)

Printed in the United States of America
Bloomington, Indiana
This book is printed on acid-free paper

Dedication

This book is dedicated to my father--- Tommy Lea. The simple love he showed the Lord Jesus and our family has made all the difference in my life.

Acknowledgement

*I want to thank those who helped in proofing and editing this book—Connie Gault (Yorktown Baptist Church), Dottie Nelson (First Baptist Church, Leesburg, Florida), Helen Dent (Southwestern Baptist Theological Seminary) and Willa McCurdy (the world's best mother-in-law).

*I also want to thank one of my mentors—Dr. Brad Waggoner for considering this book and pointing me to Cross Books. Thanks for the tremendous investment you made in my life during and since college.

*Special thanks to Matt Monroe and Phil Burgess with Cross Books. You all were a joy to work with!

*I also am so grateful to my dear mother—Beverly Lea—for her excellent writing suggestions and for helping me with some factual information about Dad. You are such a kind and wonderful mother. I love you!

*I want to thank First Baptist Church, Leesburg, Florida for being such a supportive and loving congregation. Thank you for calling me to serve you and for being a group of people that are hungry for God's word.

*To my boys---Nate, Luke, Joseph, Tommy and Stephen. I tried to write this book when you all were asleep or at school. I love you guys so much that I hurt when I think about it. I wanted to tell you 4 things: 1) I love you 2) God loves you 3) You are great sons 4) You are created for God's Glory

*Last of all, I want to thank my lovely bride and best friend—Suzy. I have not gotten over you! You are God's gift to me--- my miracle and perfect complement. Where would I be without my Suz?

Table of Contents

Introduction: How I Gave My Heart Away to My Dad xv

Chapter 1: Know God 1

Chapter 2: Spend Time with God 7

Chapter 3: Pursue Purity 13

Chapter 4: Manage Anger Well 21

Chapter 5: Be Interruptible 27

Chapter 6: Honor Your Parents 33

Chapter 7: Love Your Spouse 39

Chapter 8: Be Kind and Happy 47

Chapter 9: Be Home When You Are Home 53

Chapter 10: Build Relationships with Your Children 57

Chapter 11: Be Honest 65

Chapter 12: Be Accepting 71

Chapter 13: Love the Lost 77

Chapter 14: Trust God 83

Chapter 15: Be Authentic 89

Chapter 16: Die Well 95

Chapter 17: Live for God's Glory 101

Chapter 18: A Closing Challenge to Men 107

Introduction

How I Gave My Heart Away to My Dad

Dear Dad,

I was thinking of you today when I read this Proverb: **My son, give me your heart,and let your eyes observe my ways.** *(Proverbs 23:26, NIV). I just wanted you to know that long ago I gave my heart to you…and that my eyes have and still are looking to your ways. Thanks for the great example you have been to me. I continue to pray for your healing.*

Love,
Son

Billy Graham, Hudson Taylor, George Mueller, George Whitfield, William Carey, and D.L. Moody. History is filled with great men of God whose lives we would love to emulate. Some of them are so remarkable that we feel helpless in following their footsteps. From a historical Christian perspective, my dad—Dr. Tommy Lea—was certainly not one of those great men. Yet to me, he was a hero. Dad went to be with the Lord on July 2, 1999, after a four-and-a-half-year battle with cancer. He taught me innumerable things through his life. What inspires me most is that God is still using him to teach me many things even after his death.

The note above is a close version of an e-mail I sent my father a few months before his death. I had read the book of Proverbs many times before I noticed that verse tucked away in the twenty-third chapter. What did Solomon mean when he asked his son to "give me your heart"? What did it mean for me as a young man in my twenties to *"give my heart"* to my father?

I knew that verse could not have meant anything that would put our earthly fathers above the Lord. We are told to love the Lord with *all* our hearts (Mark 12:30). We are told to set apart Christ as Lord of our hearts (1 Peter 3:15). Since we are to give our hearts to Jesus, how are we also to give them to our earthly fathers?

Solomon, however, spoke powerfully to his son in God's Word saying, "*Give me your heart.*" This passage describes a heart connection that flows from a deep relationship. In essence, he is saying, *"Give me the depths of who you are. I want to know you and love you. By the way, be so close to me that you actually see what I am doing. Follow my example, because I am following hard after God's ways."*

The prophet Malachi in Malachi 4:6 (the last verse of the Old Testament) prophesied that the Lord will "**turn the hearts of fathers to [their] children and the hearts of children to their fathers."** Here God says that one of the marks of a great spiritual revival is that parents, especially fathers, have a close relationship with their children. Children are not to be merely produced, brought forth, taught, provided for, and sent off. Parents, especially the father according to these verses, are to put energy into nurturing a lasting heart relationship with their children.

When I first read those words from Proverbs 23:26, I was overcome with gratitude to God. My dad never said to me, "Hey, son, give me your heart." But he always made me feel that he wanted to be around me. He went out of his way to show me that I was important to him. He also lived a life that made me thirst for the likeness of Jesus. Therefore, I freely chose to "give him my heart" because of the life that he lived.

Now that I have the great honor of being a father, I long for my children to give their hearts to me. This verse has become the most important task for me in the complicated world of parenting. It inspires me above all else to aim for the hearts of my five sons. I am praying that this verse would be a wake-up call to Christian fathers. It is a call for a deep heart search. Are we living the kind of lives in which we truly can say to our children, "My son (or daughter), give me your heart"?

I often use something my father said or did as an illustration in my sermons. I often get teary-eyed when I mention him due to the strong emotions his memory continues to stir in me. One time a younger man in our congregation said to me, "Cliff, whenever you speak about your father, there are two people that are crying every time. One of them is you! The other one is me. I never had what you have...but I always wanted it."

This book is not something I initially wanted to write. Yet as God began to impress on me these things I was learning from Dad after his death, I began to notice how many people in my church and how many friends of mine were hurting and profoundly affected as adults by an incomplete relationship with their earthly fathers. I then felt led by the Lord to offer a brief glimpse into my relationship with my dad to share some of his traits that inspire, stretch, and instruct me today.

The key to my relationship with my father is that I gave him my heart. He wanted my heart...and he was a trustworthy person to care for it. I pray that hearing some of his investment in my life will inspire a new generation of fathers who can say with confidence to their children, *"My son, give me your heart."*

Chapter 1

Know God

Dad was a Bible scholar. For more than twenty years, he taught Greek and the New Testament at one of the world's largest seminaries. During the last five years of his life, he was the seminary's dean of the School of Theology. His library was massive. There seemed to be few subjects in the realms of theology and the Bible that he did not have a precise comment about. To me, he was like an endless gold mine of Bible answers. Yet for all his learning, I was always impressed at how Dad maintained a simple love for the gospel of Jesus Christ. He never lost the wonder of how great it was to know God in a personal way.

Dad loved the simple story about how sinners could be made right with God through faith in Christ. One time he preached at the church I was attending when I was a college student. This great professor of the New Testament preached on James 2:19 [19] **You believe that God is one; you do well. The demons also believe—and they shudder.**. He gave a simple talk about the nature of saving faith and encouraged the lost to place their faith in Christ alone for salvation. I remember people talking about that sermon for months afterward. There is something powerful about the simplicity of the gospel.

I think Dad's appreciation of the straightforward gospel message stemmed from his own experience of growing up as a child without ever truly hearing the gospel. Dad was raised in a warm, churchgoing home in Columbus, Mississippi. Though he was raised in church, the church in which he grew up did not emphasize a personal relationship with Christ. At twelve years of age, he and his friends went through a confirmation class that taught them the major tenants of the church. At the end of the class, the children were presented before the church. They recited some things they learned in the class, declared the beliefs they were taught, and officially became members of the church.

One day Dad told me of this experience. He confessed that though he and his friends could recite some doctrines of the church, they had no idea of what it meant to truly know Christ in their hearts. They may have formally been inducted as members of their church, but they had no vital relationship with God through faith in Christ.

God graciously began creating a deeper spiritual interest in my father. When he was fifteen years old, he began attending an interdenominational Bible study that met in various local homes. When he began actually studying the Bible, poring over its truths, he became convicted of his lostness and his need for Jesus. After reading God's Word and hearing the gospel, he placed his faith in Christ and invited Christ to be his Lord and

Savior. A number of teenagers shared this same experience in his town, while other saved teenagers began to grow in the Lord. My mother recounts that this Bible study was truly a great work of God in the little town of Columbus. Being saved changed my dad's life. He began to grow in the Lord and sought to emphasize the need for the gospel at his home church.

After receiving a scholarship to Mississippi State University, he completed his bachelor of science degree in electrical engineering. While he was there, he also did some preaching on the weekends in some of the smaller surrounding towns. Dad's burden to see others experience salvation in Christ grew during this time. Toward the end of Dad's college career, God made it clear to him that he was calling Dad into full-time Christian ministry. What God began in a little Bible study during Dad's teenage years was now directing the course of his life.

Salvation continued to be an important theme in Dad's life. He actively shared his faith in the settings in which God placed him. When he and Mom became parents, they desperately wanted their three children to have a personal relationship with Christ. I remember Dad saying to me, "The most important decision of your life is the decision to accept Christ." As in many evangelical homes, the topics of God, the gospel, and all things spiritual were pretty common. Being the youngest of three, by the time I was about six years old, both of my sisters had accepted Christ and followed the Lord in believer's baptism.

As a pastor's kid, unless I was having brain surgery or a heart transplant (which incidentally never happened), I was always in church. Three things were certain on Sunday mornings as I sat in the pew waiting for the service to end: I was fidgety; I yearned for attention; and I loved watching my dad preach. When I was about seven years old, these things collided at the end of the service almost every week. When Dad finished his sermon, he began to invite people to come forward to receive Christ into their lives. I regularly remember the music leader singing several verses of the hymn "Just As I Am." Dad would implore people to come forward and receive the good news of Christ, inviting him full access to their lives.

I remember itching to go forward to talk to Dad for weeks on end. My mom was not bashful about telling me that she did not think I was ready. If I continued to plead and protest, I received the classic "church pinch." Ouch! It still hurts to think about it. There was a battle between us about my motives for wanting to go forward at the end of the service. She knew I was a "ham" and that I loved being with my dad—even if it meant a premature altar call. She wisely resisted my doing something publicly that I did not understand.

I have some memory still about my parents talking to me about Jesus at home during those days. They told me about his death, my sin, the cross, and the wonderful victory of the resurrection. As an eight-year-old boy, I didn't understand much. But I understood I needed Christ. With great eagerness, I prayed and invited Jesus Christ into my life. Then, I finally went forward and talked to Pastor Dad at the end of a service. A few months later, I was baptized by my dad. The memory would forever linger in my mind as I stood with Dad in the warm water in front of 500 people. It was way better than getting pinched by my mom and listening to a long sermon. At last my parents felt I understood what I was doing. I rejoice that God saved me, and I began a relationship with him.

Since I received Christ at such a young age, I occasionally had doubts about my salvation as a teenager. I began to see that my uncertainties usually occurred either during times when I was not growing stronger in my relationship with God or during times when I was tempted to trust in an "experience" of salvation rather than truly in Christ.

One evening during my freshman year of college, I was helping out as a counselor at a youth camp. There was a fiery, stirring evangelistic message that urged kids to make sure they were saved and were going to heaven when they died. All of a sudden, I was not sure. The memory of my praying and receiving Christ with my parents had somewhat faded in my mind. I found the nearest pay phone (that was a long time ago, long before cell phones) and called my parents. My dad put me at rest like he often did. He assured me that he felt I understood what I was doing when I received Christ. The Lord used my dad to comfort me with the truth of my salvation. I was to trust in the Lord, not in an experience. Christ is my salvation, not a prayer I barely remember saying with my parents when I was a kid. As I prayed over the verse Romans 8:16, the Holy Spirit began to testify strongly to my spirit that I was indeed his child. I needed much growth. But by his grace, I was assured that I had received Christ in my life as a young child.

Dad was right. The *most important* decision I ever made was to receive Christ in my life. It was also *the best* decision I ever made. I praise God that he drew me to himself and inspired me to believe in him. I also praise God that knowing God is the beginning, not the end, of the story.

Chapter 2

Spend Time with God

Knowing God was not an event for my father. It was a lifetime goal and pursuit. When my father preached at my ordination service a few months before he died, he challenged me and our church to make the goal of our lives to know God. He preached from Philippians 3:8, which says, **I also consider everything to be a loss in view of the surpassing value of knowing Christ**[B] **Jesus my Lord.**

Knowing God is to be our life. Knowing God was Dad's life. The primary way that my Dad developed his heart for knowing God was to simply spend time alone with God. There was no flashy plan or wild new idea for him; just meet with God each day with consistency, honesty, and transparency.

I never liked to get up exceptionally early as a kid. Yet it seems that any time I was awake before 6:30 am, I would find my dad praying and seeking the Lord. He wore a maroon bath-robe, old brown house shoes, and black horn-rimmed reading glasses. I'd find him sitting on a couch in our living room reading beneath the light of a lamp. He would look up at me with a warm glance, and I would think to myself, "That is crazy to be up this early. Is the Lord even up yet?"

Yet this was my dad's habit. He spent time alone with God absorbed in his Word and prayer every day. As I think of Dad's devotional life, two words come to mind: discipline and desire. There is a vital balance between those two traits that we must find to experience real progress and joy in the Christian life.

Discipline described Dad to the hilt. He watched what he ate. He watched how he spent money. He exercised. He seemed to have an almost unnatural control over the desires of his flesh.

I found it interesting one day when Dad told me the story of a former college roommate who noticed Dad's strong, disciplined devotional habits. One day his roommate said, "Tommy, would you pray for me to get up and spend time with God?"

Dad told his roommate, "Don't ask me to pray for you to get up. Just wake up." That was how Dad thought.

I remember hearing Dad teach on the verse "*train yourself to be godly*" (1 Timothy 4:7). He felt spiritual growth was a gift of God's grace. But this growth did not occur without an intentional, disciplined pursuit. When he retreated into the living room to be with God, he brought with him Peter Lord's *2959* prayer book and his Greek New Testament. As a young seminary student, he learned to master the Greek New Testament. It never hit me until I was a seminarian just how amazing it was for someone to read devotionally from the Greek Bible. I wish I could have inherited that ability through osmosis. The *2959* prayer book was a popular prayer guide that encouraged people to write down a list of prayer concerns and methodically pray for 30 minutes (*29 minutes and 59 seconds*) every day. That was what worked for Dad, and he stuck with it for years.

As he prayed and read the Word, he asked God to fill him with spiritual power for the busy day of ministry ahead. He shared with me that he was intentional not to use this time to study for sermons or for his lectures at the seminary. This was his time to be alone with his Maker. Dad was disciplined. Yet it was a discipline coupled with something equally as powerful: *desire to know God.* I still remember how passionately he preached my ordination sermon. He talked about "Knowing God." I distinctly remember one of his favorite sayings: "The most important thing in this life is for us to know God." That is why he spent time with God. Dad simply wanted to get to know him better.

In Dad's workbook called *God's Transforming Word*, he wrote a very simple statement that says, "If your life is to be transformed through Bible study, you must have a spiritual hunger for God's Word" (page 7). That is what I noticed in Dad. He was not seeking merely to check off a list of spiritual duties he had to accomplish each day to stay in good favor with God. He pursued biblical study and a fervent prayer life to build a relationship with God because he was truly hungry to be with God. Alone time with God for many Christians sounds boring, legalistic, and for the most part bogged down with distractions and inconsistent efforts. Dad kept consistent because of desire.

One example of this desire was evident on family vacations. We were one of those families that would get up bright and early to go out of town. When we climbed into the car, everyone but Dad would go to asleep. As Mom woke up, he would ask her to read God's Word to him while he drove. Why did Dad do this? I never sensed it was because he had to. It was not because he was a minister and he would feel guilty if he did not have his "quiet time." His sincere desire was that he really wanted to be alone with God. His day was not right without the Word of God pumping through his heart.

I noticed this same thing during my dad's final battle with cancer. My dad's battle with cancer was long…but his illness was debilitating for only about the last month of his life. He spent most of that time in the hospital. I had the joy of spending several nights alone with him. One morning as I was quietly reading my Bible, he whispered to me, *"Son, would you pass me my Bible?"* He was very weak and broken at this point. I was so proud of this hurting servant of Jesus who wanted to talk and commune with his master…even though he would be with him eternally in heaven in just a few short days. He wanted to stay close to his Creator even on his deathbed. I will never forget how this deeply sick man was hungry for God.

We also talked about Scripture memory that day in the hospital. Dad was in the habit of memorizing long portions of Scripture. He had put Ephesians, 1 Peter, and other books to memory. I asked Dad what he was reading that morning. He said that he had recently had been trying to memorize the Pastoral Epistles (1 and 2 Timothy and Titus). Weakness etched lines in his face that I had never seen before as he said that. I said something to the effect of, "Dad…take it easy. You can take a break from memorizing those three books of the Bible." He did not want to. He had desire.

There was something else that authenticated Dad's devotional life. This may sound strange…but Dad *looked* like he spent time with God. There was freshness about his demeanor that communicated that his "devotions" did not end when he got up from the couch. He kept the conversation with God going throughout the day. We talked several times about Brother Lawrence's classic book, *The Practice of the Presence of God.* This book talks about how to make your life a constant conversation with God. Dad tried to connect his devotions with his day. His life was merely an outflow of that alone time with the Lord.

Why did Dad's devotional life have a profound impact on me? It was not because Dad looked at me one day and said, "Son, you have been saved for several years now. Why don't you start acting like your mother and me and get up and read your Bible each morning?" That would have likely injected a ritualistic guilt into me. I never recall him or my mom urging me or coercing me to read the Bible. We had family devotions fairly consistently. We prayed before meals…but I felt no pressure from him to copy his habits. Dad's example of spending time with God simply made me hungry. When I was thirteen years old, God began to close in on me and work in me a thirst for his Word like Dad had.

In the eighth grade, I was blessed to have a Sunday school teacher who was a seminary student and who took an unusual interest in me. His influence was a God-ordained and blessed complement to Dad's influence. I was reluctant when he started telling a rowdy group of eighth graders in Sunday school to start spending time with God each day. Then, he challenged me. I couldn't back down from a challenge. Likely just to meet the proposed challenge, I began doing it. I decided to get up every day and begin spending time with God in prayer and in the Bible whether I felt like it or not. I struggled to make it a powerful, intimate time. I also was too focused at first on "doing it and getting it done" rather than actually seeking to strengthen my relationship with God. Yet in time God made this duty of spending time with him a true delight.

Today, I get fidgety and feel queasy inside if I have not had a proper intake of God's Word. God worked in me a "gotta have it" feeling toward spending time with him. I want to grow in it still. I want daily to be like Jeremiah when he said in Jeremiah 15:16, "**Your words were found, and I ate them. Your words became a delight to me and the joy of my heart,**

So shall it be for us all. God is working this in me by his grace…and largely because of the disciplined thirst I first saw in my dad.

Chapter 3

Pursue Purity

I was a seminary student at Southwestern Baptist Theological Seminary in Fort Worth when my dad was the dean of the School of Theology. I was able to have him as a professor for only a couple of one-week classes between semesters. Those times of sitting under his teaching are a treasure to me.

One class I took from him was on the Pastoral Epistles (1 and 2 Timothy and Titus). One day, I remember him teaching on a call to holiness from Timothy. It was from 2 Timothy 1:9, which says that God "**has saved us and called us with a holy calling**

My dad urged the men and women in the class to pursue purity and live lives of holiness. Then he shared something personal and profound with the class. He said that when he was a young child, some of his friends had some pornographic magazines. Though he was not a ringleader in looking at the magazines, he shared that he had seen a few pictures. Then he said, "Because of what I saw in those magazines when I was child, I have been very careful ever since about what I allow my eyes to see."

I praise the Lord that my dad did not have a problem with pornography. I believe the reason he did not is because he was proactive in preventing it. That day he told our class that unless we are careful, we will all be governed by our senses and live lives of impurity. He was opening up to his students saying that even the dean of the School of Theology could be prone to look at impure things if he were to let his guard down.

The fascinating thing to me about his comments that day was that I had never known he even thought about letting his guard down. His guard seemed to be constantly up. He desired to be a pure vessel before the Lord. That guard for purity was a constant challenge to me.

Occasionally he challenged me with a pep-talk about his own experiences. I was impacted one day when he told me, "Cliff, I have never smoked anything, drank anything, or taken any drug." The context of his statement was not one of arrogance. Neither was his statement a way of saying that abstinence from these things equals holiness or that Christians who responsibly drink alcohol or use tobacco are not holy. He was simply telling me that he had had a wonderful life without messing with any of those things. It fascinated me to the point of wanting to be able to say the same thing to my children. By the grace of God, I am able to say the same thing. Merely abstaining from wrong things was not the end of purity for my father. Nor can it be for us. But it is certainly part of the battle.

A friend recently shared with me that he had my dad for class at seminary. He described that day Dad first walked into class. Everyone's eyes followed him. He dropped his books on the table and said, "Let's pray." He went into a prayer that focused on praying for holiness and purity. My friend said that people were both convicted of sin and deeply challenged in their personal lives just from that prayer. This was a natural manifestation of Dad's passion for purity.

He also was open with me about sexual issues. I was the only kid I knew who had a descriptive talk with his father about several sexual issues pertinent to men. When Dad talked to me about the issues and experiences that stem from an adolescent's lustful imagination, I did not know what he was talking about. Dad wanted to inform me of experiences he had as a kid, things that I was about to be tempted with and the dangers in my life that could come by being sucked into sexual impurity.

These talks did a couple of things: they bonded my heart closer with my father, and they took away any curiosity in me to experiment with sexual sin. When I was a university minister for several years, I regularly talked with young men who struggled with addiction to pornography and the ensuing sexual effects it brings. For most of the guys, I was the first person who ever talked with them candidly on that subject. Oh, how I wished that these hurting young men had fathers who talked to them in the way my dad did! A host of tears and sorrows could truly have been spared.

Purity was something that mattered to him. He had a way of pointing me to purity and not letting me disrespect him. I remember being into the fad of having posters line the walls of my bedroom when I was a kid. It was an '80s thing. I was (and am) a big sports fan. I remember having an impressive poster of NBA great George Gearvin on my wall. I was at a friend's house who lived nearby. He wanted to trade me something for my George Gearvin poster. He offered me the trade of George Gearvin for a swimsuit poster of Farrah Fawcett. I figured it was a fair trade. I thought since I never got to watch *Charlie's Angels* because it was on Sunday evening during church, this would be a great way to keep up with some of the show's characters.

I brought the poster home and sneaked it up on the wall in my room. The main thing I remember about what transpired in the next few hours at home was that my deal did not go so well. Farrah was not going to work in my dad's house. That poster was gone by sundown. (I can't remember if I ever got George Gearvin back.)

Many might also remember those long-gone inventions called "records." My friends and I would often go to the mall on Saturdays and head straight for the record store where I would often buy a '45 single with one song on the front and one song on the back. One day, for some reason, I bought a rock song that had a sexually suggestive title. Later that day, my dad caught a glimpse of the title, and that was the end of that. My dad told me I needed to break that record (that I just paid two bucks for) in half. I grudgingly broke the record in his presence.

What sticks out to me now about these incidents is that Dad was not going to allow his son to go unchallenged by him in the battle for purity. He had written a discipleship booklet on the book of Ephesians. He was all too familiar with Ephesians 5:3 that says, **sexual immorality and any impurity or greed should not even be heard of among you**

In a world where we are bombarded with blatant sexuality at every turn, Dad said to me, "We are not even going to hint at sexual immorality." And somehow, he kept his relationship with me so tight that I trusted rather than resented his actions.

Though he challenged me with his words, Dad mostly challenged me in purity with his life. I was not immune to sexual temptation as a teenager. I remember facing sexual temptation like any young man did. Something very hard to explain happened to me on several occasions repetitively. If I were in a situation where I was even slightly tempted to engage in immorality, I would often literally see an image of Dad's face appear in my mind. When tempted toward sexual sin, Dad's physical face would pop up. A glance of his face, glowing with Christ's purity and his love for me, drew me to run to Christ. "Looking at Dad" was a powerful deterrent to escape the lies of acting on my sexual impulses.

Though Dad's example was a powerful force in my battle for purity, God still impressed on me that my main motives for purity must be Godward. After all, Paul tells us clearly in 1 Thessalonians 4:3 that **For this is God's will, your sanctification: that you abstain from sexual immorality**

For the glory of God we say "no" to the natural and evil inclinations of our sinful nature. Like Joseph in Genesis 39:9, when tempted toward sexual sin we must say, **So how could I do such a great evil and sin against God?"**

But for many today, God is completely factored out of the equation when it comes to sexual desire. We continue to cave and give in because our desires trump a desire to honor God in this all-important area of sexuality.

The truth is, we have God's power to live at a high level of purity today. We are told in Ephesians 5:3 not to have even a "hint" of sexual immorality in our lives. Then we are told in 2 Peter 1:3 that in Christ we have "everything we need for life and godliness." When I read that Americans are buying and renting some 800 million pornographic videos a year, it is clear that we are far to the north of hinting at sexual sin. But if we truly believe God's Word, we will believe that God can empower us to live free from sexual sin's rule.

Part of the tool to fight sexual sin that Dad modeled was that he always treated everyone, especially ladies, with respect. Treating ladies with honor is a great weapon to battle the temptation toward purity. I recently met with a young man who had struggled for years with pornography addiction and sexual sin. The young man said he was serious about God and even felt a call to ministry, but was racked by shame and defeat in this area of his life. I encouraged him to have a renewed zeal to be free from this particular stronghold. He did not seem to be hearing me, so I told him how poorly he was treating women by viewing pornography. I even said to him, "If you do not quit looking at pornography, you are likely to rape or murder someone." He got the point. 1 Thessalonians 4:5 says that we should learn to control our bodies in a way that is holy and honorable. Engaging in lewd pictures is the opposite of God's heart from that verse.

I remember how enraged I was at a Fort Worth gas station a few years ago when my seven–year-old son was with me.

There was a man buying a "behind-the-counter" pornographic magazine in front of me. There were also pictures of bikini-clad women in various parts of the gas station. The air in the place was thick with evil. I was so bothered that I thought it was time to have one of those "talks" with my son. As he and I were driving back home I said, "Son, did you notice that there were magazines behind the counter at that gas station...and some pictures of girls in bathing suits in other parts of the store?"

"Yeah. I think so, Dad," my son said.

"Well, Nate, this may surprise you, but some of those magazines behind the counter have pictures of girls with no clothes on," I went on to explain. Nathan's face contorted into a "yuck" expression of disbelief. As we talked about it further, I emphasized that some men who do not follow God's ways look at magazines like that. It shows that they do not respect God or women. As we talked further about the respect issue, I became afraid that he might go home and tell his younger brothers about the naked lady magazines at the gas station. So I said to him, "Nate, I don't think your brothers are ready to hear about this stuff you and I talked about today."

He said, "Dad, don't worry about that. I never want to talk about this again." I had to laugh. I am known for going overboard in talking about these matters to the boys. Though he had certainly had enough, I think he was starting to get the point about the importance of purity and treating ladies with honor.

Occasionally I get a little help in the pursuit of purity from my wife. My wife often works out with one of those exercise balls. She has an exercise video to assist her in her workouts.

The video is taught by a guy who looks like Richard Simmons without the hairdo. On one of the videos he is surrounded by what you might call "lovely assistants" wearing tight workout clothes. I have never closely seen exactly what these ladies look like. The reason for that is because whenever I am walking through the room when my wife is using that video, she tells me, "You do not need to look at the screen right now." I wasn't sure why when she first said this to me. She explained that a close look at these well-toned ladies would not be good for any man to see.

I think men especially need to take all the help they can get in the pursuit of purity. Though I am imperfect in all my pursuits, my dad's example gave me an interest in aiming to live at a high level of purity. *"Blessed are the pure in heart."*

Chapter 4

Manage Anger Well

The Bible says, **A fool gives full vent to his anger, but a wise man holds it in check.**(Proverbs 29:11).

One of the most freeing and wonderful things about my childhood is that I have few memories of my dad being angry. Quite honestly, I have to work overtime to conjure even a few instances where Dad raised his voice or lost his cool. Even the ones that come to mind are minor and seem clearly a result of my foolishness. Oh, for more homes where that is the case!

Yet as I reflect on Dad as an adult, I am certain that he felt the normal emotion of anger many times. When Paul told us in Ephesians 4:26 not to sin in our anger, I think that implies that not all anger is sin. Christ was famously angry at sin when people were using the temple as a haven for deceptive financial schemes (Matthew 21:12–13). David was overcome with anger at sin when he declared in Psalms 119:53, **Rage seizes me because of the wicked who reject Your instruction.** It is a joy to look back on how my father dealt with the emotion of anger to recall that the memories I have of his anger either involve a righteous display of fury or a well-governed response of anger.

One memory that sticks out to me occurred as an early teenager watching the Grammy Awards. Dad did not watch a great deal of television but would often bring a book to "his chair" in the living room where the family would be watching TV. A certain R&B singer (I am not going to use any names here...but I will say that this person was formerly known as "The Artist") was receiving an award for vocalist of the year. This singer was not known for Bible studies and gospel songs. He was known for sexually explicit lyrics and lewd behavior.

He had just performed a sexually charged song that I believe my dad caught the tail end of. When he went to receive his award, the singer said, "First of all, I want to thank my Lord and Savior Jesus Christ." Dad looked up and got unusually red-faced. I suppose I have never seen him this angry. He said something to the effect of, "That is wrong! I feel like Joshua!"

That sort of took the fun out of the Grammys for us kids. I think a subtle channel change is what happened next. Dad never fully explained why he felt like Joshua. He just let it sit there and sink into our minds. I have since read the book of Joshua many times. My guess is that Dad felt like Joshua did when he challenged the people who wanted to worship idols yet still claim and worship the one true God. Joshua was tired of their lukewarm attitude and said to God's people, **choose for yourselves today the one you will worship** (Joshua 24:15). Dad was angry because he loved God and had devoted his life to seeing people live out the fullness of their faith in him. For this perverse singer to play the "Jesus is cool" card and then continue to sow his wild oats and pray for crop failure was anger-inducing to Dad.

There were other things that could raise his emotions and show signs of human anger. You know what I recall frustrated him most? In my memory, it was when I did not take good care of things at the house. Though Dad was far from being a "fanatic" about his stuff, he had a strong desire to teach me responsibility about things for which he had worked hard. One of the few angry moments I remember about him was when he was in my room and noticed that I had made a mark or small hole on my wall. When he asked me about it, I shrugged off the wall blemish as if it were no big deal. Dad said something sternly to me along the lines of, "Son, you need to learn to take better care of this house!" He left the room shortly after that. The tone he used was not overly harsh, but different than how he normally spoke to me. Within a matter of minutes, he came back to me to check on me and apologized for how he expressed himself. That is the heart of well-expressed anger. It does not mean that you never use a different tone. It is about keeping your relationships. It's about being humble enough even to go to your child and say, "Hey. Are we all right? I did not mean to express myself like that. I love you, son."

He also had an inviting way of teaching me about anger. I had to watch my temper as a boy. I was sometimes explosive, but usually I would just get irritable and express my anger in a poor fashion. The most vivid memory I have about Dad teaching me to manage anger well is when we were playing racquetball.

There were days he would take me to the seminary recreational center (the RAC) to play racquetball. Dad played regularly with some of his colleagues, so he was fairly proficient at the game. As he was teaching me to play, I just wanted once to get close to beating him. After I realized I was a long way from beating him any time soon, I would get angry at the bad shots I made and the good ones that he made.

Dad was patient with my moaning. But I began to form a habit of whining about the outcome of the game. Dad looked at me and said a typical, universal "Dad" statement to me one time. But for some reason it sunk in, embedded a permanent memory in my mind. He said, "Son, do you realize that it is no fun for either of us when you act like that?" I thought about it but didn't say much. Looking back, it was that statement that God used to begin to curb my anger problem. I began to see the futility of expressing my anger that way. The more I thought about it, I realized that he was right. I was not having any fun, and I could have been. I saw firsthand the beauty of the calm, governed spirit of my dad. I began to crave that. I was frustrated with my emotions governing me. It motivated me to believe that **A fool gives full vent to his anger,** (A) [a] **but a wise man holds it in check.** (Proverbs 29:11).

I still see the temptation to anger. As I was reading through the Old Testament one time, I remember being hit hard with the verse from Ecclesiastes 7:9, **Don't let your spirit rush to be angry, for anger abides in the heart of fools.** I liked the simplicity of that verse. A few years ago after reading that verse, it made me think about one of my sons who struggled with a quick temper. I decided I was going to ask God to set him free from a spirit of anger, so I began to pray that verse for my son. What I noticed as I prayed that verse for my son was that I really still needed to pray that verse for myself. I saw that many times I was quick to anger and sour in my tone. Praying that verse for my son was God's conviction and reminder that I should pray that verse for myself and seek to continue to manage anger well for God's glory.

Proverbs 12:16 says, **A fool's displeasure is known at once, but whoever ignores an insult is sensible.** We are so easily angered. The Bible does not sugarcoat that situation and habit. It simply says that it is foolish! One time my family was visiting my in-laws in their home in Albuquerque, New Mexico. Fireworks are legal in their city limits. So we were lighting them in celebration of the New Year. My wife was understandably uncomfortable when I let my four-year-old light a few of the fireworks. I tried to tell her that it was safe because there was a long fuse. Incidentally, I learned that night that there was not a fuse long enough for a mother to feel safe with her four-year-old lighting firecrackers.

As I was thinking on that incident, the Lord reminded me that I will be safe and my family will be safe when I (and when we all) have very long fuses. Spirits that are quickly provoked and attitudes that show our annoyance at once are dangerous for our spiritual and relational health. When I feel the pressure of life tempting me to be surly in my tone and demeanor, I pray for a long fuse, remember God's truth in his Word about anger, and reflect of the vivid example of how Dad had God-honoring anger that was controlled, well timed, and rightly expressed.

Chapter 5

Be Interruptible

"Pastor Cliff, I am so sorry to call you at home. I know you are so busy with all of those boys, but I just need to ask you one thing."

I have heard statements like that for years. Honestly, I rarely mind being contacted in that way. But we all come across people that cannot stand to have their private world or their focused schedule open to the slightest amount of distraction. Picture someone in your mind who has a large responsibility. Your attempts at communicating with them have been uncomfortable. You grow nervous to "impose" on them because they appear stressed, overly-focused, and unwilling to be deterred from their pursuits. What if that person happens to be your father? That is certainly not how you want to come across if you are a parent. That kind of demeanor and persona communicates lethal things to your children.

Interruptible is one of the best ways I can describe my father. He was open to interruptions from his family, colleagues, and especially the Lord. Dad had a small study in his room. I never felt like he spent too much time there, but he was regularly there in the evenings studying or taking care of bills. If I ever needed anything from him, my recollection is that I felt completely free to go see him. I usually did not have great reasons to go in there. But I *always* felt welcome to interrupt him.

I remember coming into his study at times with odd things to say. When I was around nine years old, I was having a hard adjusting to our recent move from Alabama to Texas. We moved from Birmingham, where Dad was a pastor, to Fort Worth, where he became a seminary professor. The move was not what I thought it was going to be. Though it seems nothing now, I went through a period in which I missed my friends, neighborhood, and church back in Alabama.

I had done some thinking one day. I somberly approached Dad in his study and said, "Dad, I need to talk." Dad glanced up and looked right at me and said, "Go ahead, son."

I proceeded, "I have decided what I want to do when I grow up." Dad kept his eyes fixed on me as he listened closely. "Dad, I want to work at my favorite restaurant, *Shoney's,* during the day and *Baskin-Robbins* at night. Except on Wednesday nights and Sunday. That way I can attend church at our old church."

He smiled (probably trying hard not to laugh) and said something like, "Son, that is great. You might change your mind and there is no need to rush into this, but that is great." I left thinking my future was bright and clear. I was going to work at my two favorite eating establishments as a career and move back to Alabama! I laugh when I think about that story. But my heart is warmed as I think about a dad who listened to me. A dad who put his book down, who put his world down... and crawled into mine for a moment to listen to my wild ideas. He did not belittle my ideas, but listened.

Being interruptible was also something Dad seemed to cultivate in his own relationship with God. When I was in my mid-twenties, Dad and I were having a talk about some things that God was teaching us. That is frankly an unusual, but tremendous, conversation for a child to have with a parent. I never even came close to thinking of Dad as a "peer." But for a son and father to share mutually what the Lord was doing in our lives showed some meekness and vulnerability on his part that amazed me.

One of the things he told me was that God was teaching him to be more open to interruptions in his life. As a busy, hard-working minister, he had been convicted by God that he needed to be open to daily "interruptions" by the Lord. He was basically saying that he often had his day planned out and that he did not receive unscheduled events as well as he wanted to. He was asking God to teach him to be more interruptible. That got the attention of this young minister! My prayer was, "Living God, make me open to your moment-by-moment directives."

As I read the gospels, I see Jesus having this same ability to be interruptible. On his way to one healing, he would stop to help someone else. He knew what he was doing but was always open to help another hurting soul in need.

All of us have been around someone that we viewed as stiff, aloof, and uninterested in us talking to them. After a while we have very little interest in being around that person. They are not interested in us, and even if that person is special to us, we wear out on putting forth energy into them. A child can "wear out" on breaking through the ice of a cool father very early in life.

I think about my dad at night when my five kids are supposed to be in bed. Inevitably one of them has a question or has trouble sleeping. "*Dad!*" I have just started talking to my wife or attending to something I really wanted to get to. I often feel like saying, "What do you want? Go to sleep…I will talk to you in the morning if you are lucky." I do not want to answer them, but my "interruptible father" comes to mind.

One time one of my sons called me in his room and asked me, "Dad, why are marshmallows white?" I really did not have the answer to that one. But my memory of a patient, listening father often trumps my natural inclination to pop off with something like, "Sugar is white because God made it white. Marshmallows have sugar in them…now go to sleep!"

I also think about this trait of my dad when I am working. I love being a pastor. I love the variety and challenge as well as the actual duties. I often write lists of things I am going to do for the day. I like crossing things off the list. It did not take me long to learn that not everything gets checked off the list so easily.

One summer a minister that my father had mentored, Dr. Gene Mims, was talking to my dad. Dad shared with him that I had gone to college and had been sensing a call to the ministry. Gene asked if I would be interested in coming to his church that summer to be a youth intern. I was thrilled for the opportunity. I remember my first day on the job: Dr. Mims met with the four youth interns. One of the things he told us was, *"In ministry, you never get it all done."* That was hard for me to hear, because I liked and still like to get things done. I think about that statement a great deal as God sends daily interruptions to my schedule. I am to view them as new opportunities from God rather than interruptions.

I am encouraged by the attitude admonished in Proverbs 8:34, **Anyone who listens to me is happy, watching at my doors every day, waiting by the posts of my doorway.**

That verse emboldens me to heed my dad's example and seek to be interruptible to the Lord.

Chapter 6

Honor Your Parents

Honor your father and your mother – Exodus 20:12

My dad was a teenager in the 1950s. That was well before James Dobson and the modern family movement. It was before there was a multitude of Christian resources to teach Christian families how to rear kids and love each other. In light of that, I am stunned at how much natural insight Dad had at being a son, husband, and father. One thing that I had not appreciated until well into my adult years involved lessons I learned from him about how to be an honorable son to my parents.

What does it mean to "honor" your parents? The concept of honor means to hold in high regard. It means to treat them as something valuable. The above commandment in Exodus had to do with children treating their parents' advice and leadership with respect and obedience. As children grow older, the specifics of how to "honor" your parents change. But I observed in my father a healthy and balanced ability to hold his parents in high regard throughout his whole life.

My dad's father was a native Mississippian. He was a gracious southern gentleman who worked for years in the railroad industry. My dad's mother was also a southern lady. She was a kind woman, but suffered often from emotional problems that to this day I do not know much about. Today we would likely say she was prone to depression and nervous breakdowns. Dad was their only child. It did not take long in their presence to know that the pride and joy of their life was their son—Tommy Lea.

If they had been rich, my dad would have likely been spoiled. I remember when I was a young boy, my grandparents could not stop talking about what a fine boy their son Tommy was. One day when I was a teenager, my grandfather (Pop) asked me, "Don't you think your father, Tommy, is a wonderful man?" I responded, "Of course, Pop. Dad is the greatest." As Pop got older, every conversation we had turned to what a wonderful man his son Tommy had become. My sisters and I would laugh out loud behind closed doors at how predictable a conversation with Pop could be: it inevitably ended up revolving around the greatness of their son Tommy.

Mr. and Mrs. Lea attended faithfully a mainline, traditional church that did not teach about having a personal relationship with Christ. My father shared the gospel with them many times. While he remained unsure about his mother's salvation, Dad rejoiced that he felt his father receive Christ into his life sometime during his nineties. So while they did not rear Dad on Dobson, and likely did not have a true relationship with

Christ, Dad was blessed to be reared in a home of such deep and authentic love.

Something that was important to my grandmother once Dad left the house was regular communication from him. My dad was a letter writer. I remember well Dad handwriting me letters when I went to college. When is the last time you wrote a real, personal letter with your hand? I think most of us e-mail junkies would say it has been some time. My father sent his parents a handwritten note in the mail every single week until they passed away in the '80s and '90s. He also called them every Saturday morning by eight o'clock. He may have felt some "pressure" to do that from them, but he never let on that it might be a burden. He seemed to gladly and seriously take on his responsibilities as an adult son.

Dad also refused to poke fun at his parents. They were wonderful people, but an easy target for a family joke. They wanted the grandkids to watch Lawrence Welk with them. They referred to butter as "oleo." They called syrup "molasses" and ice cream "cream." They wanted us (even as teenagers) to gather around the piano and sing songs like "Danny Boy." They set the breakfast table at night right after dinner was over. Sometimes they were so "ready" for us to come to the breakfast table that they had already poured the milk on our cereal. They were a hoot. But I never saw my father show them anything but respect. If we kids were cackling at their oddities, Dad would not. He still gave them "yes sirs" and "yes ma'ams," honoring them with his words and actions until they were no more. He preached at both of their funerals with power…and honored their memory with eloquence and compassion.

I have heard that Dad had to talk straight with them a few times. For some reason, my grandmother had in her mind that parents picked favorites. She only had one child. But her son had three. When I was a college student and drove through Mississippi on my way to a summer job, my grandmother asked me, "Cliff, who do you think your parents like the best? I bet it is you." I chalked her question up to possible senility and simply responded by saying, "Grandmother, my parents like all of us the same." I shared that experience with Dad. He told me that early on during our childhood, his mother said something similar to him. He stood up to her with respect and said something like, "Mother, we love all our children the same…and we would ask you to do the same." He honored her, while being clear with her. That was one thing my parents were adamant about. There was not a touch of favoritism in our home. We all got 33.33 percent of a Hershey bar…along with their love.

Some commandments are more difficult to obey than others. I am grateful that it never seemed too difficult to honor my parents. I think the main reason was that I watched my dad so patiently honor his parents. I obviously did not always agree with my parents or like every decision they made for me. I shared different perspectives on minor issues regularly. But there was something wonderful for me when I showed right honor to my parents.

Though honoring my parents seemed somewhat natural, I also know that it was something we were taught. One way my father taught me about honor was to show me that there was a line not to cross with them. One of the worst sins in the Lea household was to say "NO" to Mom or Dad. The Lea kids were allowed to express ourselves to our parents. Even if we were upset and bothered, open communication was acceptable. But there was a dear price to be paid for a defiant, rebellious "No." Highlighting that "sin" above all others drummed into us the importance of honor. Dad especially would not tolerate me talking rudely to Mom.

I need some work on this principle as a father myself. I love the individuality and the leadership potential that swims around in my five strong-willed sons. But, with their strong-willed leanings comes a tendency to think before speaking. My dear wife is an "old school" mom in that she is tireless and "hands-on" in her attention and care of the boys. Occasionally one of the boys will have the audacity to say something to Suzy like, "Why is my favorite shirt still in the dirty clothes?" Part of me wants to lash out in anger. Then other times, I may not even notice what was said because it sounds strangely normal. God is growing me in seeking to have a firm, balanced response that teaches them to honor their dear mother.

I am grateful that my dad modeled honor for me. I am praying my boys would catch the beauty of God's original intent from that commandment: *Honor your father and your mother.*

Chapter 7

Love Your Spouse

Husbands, love your wives, [(A)] just as also Christ loved [(B)] the church *(Ephesians 5:25)*

In 1997, I was at a one-day Promise Keepers conference for ministers at Prestonwood Baptist Church in Dallas. The final sermon of the day was by John Maxwell. Though I recall it to be a stirring message, I do not remember much of what he said except for one statement. As he was challenging us to be good husbands and fathers, he said, *"You can tell a lot about a man by the happiness of his wife and the respect of his children."* As a young husband and the father of a couple of babies, that statement hit me hard.

Those words could certainly be misused to make a husband's guilt multiply if his kids were ornery and his wife was despondent. A husband's job is much more than to make sure his wife is never frustrated and that his kids say in unison, "Yes, ma'am."

But in a general sense I felt those words were true, challenging, and almost frightening.

In reflecting on that statement, I thought about how happy my mother was in her relationship with Dad. She absolutely knew he loved her. It was also clear that all three of Dad's children had the utmost respect for him. There may have even been unrealistic respect at times. "Oh God," I prayed. "Grant that I might lead my home in such a way that my wife is happy in you and my kids learn the importance of respect. Make me like that, living Lord."

One could point to many reasons that wives are unhappy in our day. Stress. Fatigue. Financial pressure. A fast-paced world. Yet I believe the main reason so many wives are unhappy is the failure of their husbands to take up the commandment in Ephesians 5 to *"love their wives as Christ loved the church."* This powerful verse teaches us that the unreserved, selfless, and sacrificial love of Jesus Christ is the standard for a husband's love for his wife. This verse also implies that husbands are to be looking for ways to nourish and cherish their wives regardless of how we are treated. Some husbands poorly reason, "I will start being more loving to my wife as soon as she starts showing me a little more respect." God's Word does not make such weak concessions for our love. "Love your wife like Christ. Period," is what God's Word commands us.

Though I did not do it consciously, much of my childhood and teenage years were spent learning this verse from my father. I sometimes ask myself, "How did Dad love Mom?" Neither of my parents had what we call today the "love language" of gift giving. They did not express their love to each other by buying things, going to fancy places, or showering each other with gifts. They expressed it by their actions. Each day I saw them with my own two eyes give each other the gifts of trust, affirmation, and powerful words. I noted that Dad was so freeing to my mother. He let her be her. He let her talk and trusted her with his feelings. As I look back, I realize that he was particularly intentional to share his life, day, and work with her.

Dad was also affectionate with Mother. When we were little, my sisters and I had plenty of moments when we would cover our eyes and giggle as we watched Dad embrace Mom and kiss her. As little ones we may have acted like it was repulsive to watch them be affectionate. But I am quite sure his love for her gave us immeasurable security. We erroneously think that the best way to give stability to our children is to incessantly dote on them and make them the center of our universe. Frankly, the most certain way to give a child feelings of assuredness and a strong identity is for Dad to show sincere, regular, and obvious love to Mom.

Consistent kind words and tone were another hallmark of how Dad loved Mom. I am not exaggerating when I say that I never once saw Dad be rude to my mother. It was as if Dad held Mom in such high esteem that even if he had felt negative emotions toward her, expressing those feelings rudely to her was not an option. Rudeness in the home is like acid corrosion on a battery. A lack of kindness slowly erodes respect, love, and the mercy of Christ in the home. I sometimes weep as I recall what I saw in my home. I saw in Dad a strong, passionate heart filled with kind words, rich affection, and an unquenchable respect for his bride.

One example of Dad's encouraging words to Mom are found in the dedication page of Dad's New Testament survey textbook he finished a few years before his death. The dedication reads, *"To my wife Beverly, whose love for the study of the New Testament constantly challenges and informs me."* I was impressed with how Dad exhibited a teachable spirit in learning from her. I also like how he picked a specific strength of Mom's and went public with his affirmation.

Another expression of Dad's love toward Mom was in the area of leadership. Dad was a consistent, kind, and gentle leader. There is a great problem in our culture with male passivity in the home. Avoiding responsibility and maximizing leisure are the themes of many home lives for men. I recently noticed a well-titled marriage book called, *Husbands Who Won't Lead and Wives Who Won't Let Them.* In my pastoral ministry, I have heard many wives express to me their longing for their husband to step up the leadership in the home. Some of their comments are, "I wish my husband would just pray with me." Or, "Why won't he take the lead on training our children?" Or, "I long for him to encourage us to read the Bible or take us to church."

On another hand, there is also a group of wives that wish their husbands were not so abrasive and dictatorial in their leadership. That is what compelled me about the way Dad loved Mom. Though he held a traditional view of male leadership concerning the roles of husbands and wives, he did not talk about the importance of my mother submitting to his leadership. He was truly living out the command in 1 Peter 3:7 for husbands to **Husbands, in the same way, live with your wives showing them honor as co-heirs of the grace of life**

He was too busy loving Mom, honoring her, and living for her to be concerned with whether or not she was following him. He was always responsible about the needs of our home, yet he gently gathered Mom's input and influence along the way.

Another important hallmark of my parents' marriage that for the most part went unnoticed by me is that of commitment. They had a far-too-short thirty-seven years of committed, marital love. Though commitment in marriage is part of our country's history, many are entering into a marriage with little determination for a lifetime commitment. Christ said, **Therefore what God has joined together, man must not separate."**

(Mark 10:9). Christ defined marriage as union that he initiated...not man. Our culture actually encourages people to experience "the magic of divorce."

Divorce is referred to as a positive, growth-oriented step. People are even throwing "divorce parties" for the newly divorced to celebrate the ending of their relationship with friends and loved ones. The chasm between the world's view of marriage and Christ's command of permanence in marriage are huge...and seem to be getting larger.

I still remember hearing what divorce was for the first time. Some kid at church told me that divorce was when your mommy and daddy stop being married and one of them moves out of the house. At six years old, I did not like the sound of that divorce thing one bit. At home that night I recall Dad sitting at the dinner table. Mom was nearby. I said, "Dad, are you and Mom ever going to get a divorce?"

Dad had a look that was somewhere between great surprise and horror on his face. "Cliff, where did you get that idea?" I told him I had heard from some friends talk about divorce, and that I was hoping it was not going to happen to us. He spoke to me in the most certain and unflinching words he could muster by saying, "Cliff, your mom and I will never, ever get a divorce. We love each other very much." *What a relief!* I thought. That was the end of that. They never remotely seemed as though they would get a divorce, but hearing Dad say it so clearly and confidently gave me immeasurable security as a child.

Dad's example had a great impact on how I would view marriage and treat my wife. Dad shared with me that the second most important decision I would ever make in my life was to decide whom I would marry. I was so excited about getting married in the summer of 1992. My wife and I both attended Hardin-Simmons University in Abilene, Texas. I met Suzy McCurdy at a college church retreat the first week of my freshmen year. We remained friends for some three years before God clearly led us to begin a relationship. I had a magical time of falling in love, sensing God's leadership to marry, and preparing for the wedding. I was a starry-eyed, unrealistic dreamer to some. That did not matter to me because I was crazy in love with the soon-to-be Mrs. Suzy Lea.

It was an honor to have Dad perform our ceremony. We then settled into our small apartment in Forth Worth, Texas, for me to begin attending seminary. We had heard all the horror stories about the dreaded "first year of marriage." I had been warned by several men that this sweet French poodle wife of mine would soon turn into a Doberman pinscher during our first year of marriage. I was curious to see if we were doomed for a life of constant scrapping and conflict.

To my delight and surprise, we remained incurably in love with one another. Every single day she would think of ways to encourage me verbally. I in turn would grab her in my arms and say things to her like, "Do you have any idea what a privilege it is to be your husband? You are all I could ever dream of in a wife. How did I get you again? You are mine!" It was unrealistic, mind-boggling continual bliss in every way.

Recently I was in a small group prayer meeting and share time on a mission trip. The missionary looked at our team at the beginning of the week and asked us to share what our greatest passions in life are. What are the things in life that cause us to be the most excited and energetic? In all seriousness I said that my first passion is God. My second passion is my wife Suzy. My love for her is extremely imperfect, but by God's grace our love is real and heart-warmingly authentic.

I have wondered many times why I have experienced such marital bliss. I know the first answer is the grace of God. God has given us five children, a busy ministry, and an active home calendar. I have seen time and time again that children, busyness, and constant activity cool the jets of a marriage. I have tasted God giving us a powerful connection in the midst of an active life. It is simply God's powerful mercy that has sustained us through the years.

I believe the second greatest factor in the marriage God has given us is watching my father relate to my mom. His natural warmth for her was the greatest human impetus in strengthening my marriage. Watching Dad shower Mom with tender, consistent, beautiful love gave me some invisible wings to ride high on the delights of love for my wife.

Chapter 8

Be Kind and Happy

Two of the most common instructions parents give their children are, "*Be kind*" and "*Quit fussing.*" I know I was told those a great deal. If, by God's grace, we can become kind and joyful people, our lives are so much better in every way. Dad attracted me to his heart with a winsome kindness and an unstoppable joy that seemed to naturally flow out of his life.

I grew up at the RAC. Some friends of mine and I would often go there to swim, exercise, and have a good time. Since my last name is spelled uniquely (and correctly!), when seminary students saw my nametag, they would ask if I was related to Dr. Lea. As I affirmed that he was my father, I cannot recount the depth of affirming things I heard about Dad.

"He is my absolute favorite professor." "I love his class." "I tried hard to get him, but his class was always too full." Statements like these were in abundance. But by far, the most common state-

ments I heard about Dad from his students and colleagues had to do with his warmth, kindness, and relational abilities.

With classes up to sixty or more people at the seminary, knowing your professor personally was not always possible. Dad would linger after class to talk with students. He also worked hard to learn names. Many people commented to me about him by saying, "I can't believe he knew my name." The Scripture in Proverbs 11:17 is right when it says, *"A kind man benefits himself.* " He was intentionally good to others and Dad reaped the benefit of living a life of kindness. As one of his colleagues related to me, "If Tommy ever had an unkind thought, I never knew it."

Something else that is a treasure to me about Dad is the overflowing joy he seemed to possess. *"Rejoice in the Lord always. I will say it again: Rejoice!"* (Philippians 4:4) comes to mind when I think of Dad. In 1 Peter 1:6, Peter talked about a *"joy unspeakable and full of glory."* My dad's joy was not something he or I could explain very precisely. It was unspeakable.

Though smiling is not always a sign of true joy, it is a blessing for me that most images I have in my mind of Dad involve him smiling. He had plenty of expressions other than smiling, but those are not as prevalent in my mind. Every mental and literal picture has his strong joy-filled smile brimming from ear to ear.

Mom did not have an overbearing amount of rules for us as kids. Yet one rule I remember well that concerned Dad was, *"Children, let your father get in the door."* We loved it when Dad came home from work. There were times when my sisters and I would often attack and swarm Dad before he got in the door.

We were politely told to give the man some room. I can still picture his face coming through the door.

Surely there were days when he felt an array of emotions and may have felt like the weight of the world was on his shoulders. But all I remember is that Dad came home happy. I can only imagine the stress he had at being an author, traveling speaker, seminary professor, husband, and father of three. But I saw none of that. He was happy in the Lord. As I grow older, I see how rare it is for people to maintain authentic joy in God through life.

In reflecting on Dad's life, I can think of several things that promoted this sense of joy. *First, it was freshness in his walk with God.* Jesus said, **Ask and you will receive,** (B) **that your joy may be complete** (John 16:24). There is a connection with how much joy we have and how often we pray. Christ promised his disciples that no one could take away their joy. There is an indomitable joy that is available to the followers of Christ simply by calling on his name. Joylessness and prayerlessness are deeply connected. David says in Psalm Psalms 40:16, "**Let all who seek You rejoice and be glad in You** Dad often wore that fresh smile of one who had recently been talking with the Father.

Second, there were strong relationships with his family. This factor is a joy killer for many. I have sat through numerous counseling sessions where husbands and wives recount the pain that their marriage and parenting challenges have brought. Tension at home makes a man's mind uneasy throughout the day. It makes coming home to "his castle" a burden that he seeks to avoid. Certainly, we are admonished to rejoice in the midst of the most unsettling trials. But poor relationships in our family make rejoicing a greater challenge. Dad's family was a joy to him! I can still see his smile as he came through the door because he truly wanted to be with us. I am to model his penchant to come home happy.

Third, there was fulfillment at work. I was touched one day when I read Ecclesiastes 5:19–20, **God has also given riches and wealth to every man, and He has allowed him to enjoy them, take his reward, and rejoice in his labor. This is a gift of, for he does not often consider the days of his life because God keeps him occupied with the joy of his heart.**When you see your work as a God-called gift, you accept it with diligence. When you do this, God shows up to keep your heart occupied with his gladness. Dad exuded a satisfaction and joy in his work. He loved being a pastor. As a seminary professor he relished the opportunity to invest in young men and women headed into the ministry.

Finally, Dad also had some simple, practical habits that promoted a sense of joy in his life. He was intentional at cultivating stress relievers. He took care of himself. He was strangely disciplined in his health and fitness. He also knew when to play and get away. He did not over-commit himself. He also avoided legalism. I never heard him say, "I just need to do more for the Lord," or "I feel so guilty that I have not done this or that." He was content to please the Lord alone…because God was his righteousness. That promoted wholeness and joy in his whole life.

When I am tempted to be irritable and despondent, I often pray what David prayed in Psalms 86:4, "Bring joy to your servant, for to you, O Lord, I lift up my soul." Then I thank God for the practical example of my father being kind and happy in the Lord.

Chapter 9

Be Home When You Are Home

Whether or not you regularly watched actor and animal enthusiast Steve Irwin's encounters with wildlife, his charismatic approach to life made his death seem all the more tragic. Following Irwin's bizarre fatality from a stingray attack on September 4, 2006, a close friend paid the Crocodile Hunter an enormous compliment. John Stainton, Irwin's producing partner and longtime friend, was interviewed on CNN hours after the world heard this shocking news. In contrast to Steve Irwin's great popularity and success, Stainton said, "As good as he was at what he did, Steve was even better at being a father and husband." Imagine what would take place in our country if every man excelled more at home with marriage and fatherhood than with colleagues and clients at work.

In 1 Peter 4:7, we are told to be "clear-minded" so we can focus on the things of God. As I meet with men throughout the week, it is confirmed that we men are prone to be consumed with earning a living, providing for the future, advancing, having our egos stroked, and getting ahead. Being "clear-minded" does not fit well in our society with all its demands. That is why my father was so refreshing to be around. He truly modeled for me the power of an uncluttered mind. Before the days when men brought home their laptops, men brought home huge briefcases brimming with urgent things they did not accomplish at work, but had to get done right away. Dad had a briefcase, but I rarely noticed him opening it. When Dad was home, he truly was home.

When I was a teenager, I worked at a fast food restaurant at the mall. For some reason, the owner/manager often put us teenagers in charge at night. He would show up only on occasion to check on us. His visits were never announced. They were surprise attacks. You can imagine that whenever he showed up, we teenagers were not quite as carefree and relaxed. The boss was there now. If we were doing everything we were supposed to be doing in his absence, we still were not comfortable with his being there. We would wonder, "When is he leaving?"

Unfortunately, many homes in our country feel the same way. The family can be alive with fun, chatter, and having good times. Then someone looks out the window and sees a car in the driveway. Many wives and children begin to think or voice things like, "Oh no. Everybody be quiet. Calm down. Dad is home." The laughing and fun are stifled by a dreary, short-fused father who wants some peace and quiet in his home. As soon as he drags himself in the room, the fun is almost instantaneously rooted out. After a while, a twisted anticipation of the hope of Dad leaving enters everyone's minds.

For most of the dads I know, work and home are two very different places; many physical and emotional miles separate the two. At work dads have employees, superiors, and colleagues. At home they have a family to supervise, a clan to corral. They spend so much energy and use so many words at work that they walk through the door with a grunt and a grumbling word about the job, a criticism about the house and kids, and a gruff inquiry about dinner. The sheer absence of anything positive or encouraging makes the family long for Dad to work late, run an errand, or have a night out with the guys.

Dad was a man who always preferred to be home when he was away. He took Mom out (even if it was to Wendy's or Luby's). He took her away on special, simple trips to be alone. He was not averse to taking us to affordable fun places near our home. But his favorite place was with us at home.

I remember that we could not wait for Dad to get home. He was not staring into space, wishing he were somewhere else. Neither was he spewing negative comments that would make us wish he were leaving. He was there. He loved us. He cared. He was interested in whatever we were doing. It was the best part of the day.

Dad's arrival at home was not "all about the kids." Dad was conscientious about honoring Mom when he came home. He would greet her affectionately and simply gave her a good amount of attention. I am told that when we were little, his routine was to relieve her by taking us to the park to play when he got off work. As we were older, I remember that after a few moments Mom and Dad would get away to the back room to discuss the day. They would take walks. They were a team. He was home and interested in her.

I thought about my dad a few times early in our marriage. I remember sitting down to dinner and having a spaced-out blank stare. When my wife noticed me doing so, she said to me, "Where are you?" I remember replying something like, "I am right here, babe. Sorry. I was thinking about something at work." She could tell that I wanted to be at home with her, but I was also distracted. I purposed in my heart that I did not want to bring home a disconnected and distracted work-centered mindset. There are exceptions when I have to make calls from home and when I have to drop everything and attend to something. I try to make those as rare as possible. I also try to express my regret to my family and let them know how I do not want to be gone long because I cannot wait to come back to be with them.

I can talk about what a priority my wife and children are to me. But they will not believe my words unless there is tangible proof. I want my family to know and *feel* that outside of the Lord, they are my highest priority. Though I work hard at limiting my travel, I have to be away on occasion for conferences and mission trips. Recently I was preparing to leave home for only an overnight trip. My oldest son touched my heart when he said, "I hate it when you have to leave."

I said to him, "You cannot hate it more than I do. Son, I am going to miss you like a leg." When I am at home, I wish I could find a huge pause button to stop the world.

Men, be home when you are home.

Chapter 10

Build Relationships with Your Children

Work is a gift from God that provides great and meaningful purpose. Yet it requires continual tenacity to maintain a healthy balance between work and other priorities.

Before James Dobson founded *Focus on the Family*, he experienced the lure of time-consuming vocational success. He has recounted that there was a time as a child psychologist when the whole world opened up to him. He could have very easily lost his kids because of work. Dobson said a letter from his father captured his attention and redirected the trajectory of his life. He recalled, "It was my father who had such a great impact on me, who saw it happening. He wrote me a letter saying he was pleased by my successes, which were far beyond his expectations, but warned me that if I lost my kids, nothing else I did would matter." That letter ultimately led to his resignation from teaching at the University of Southern California in 1977 and his founding of *Focus on the Family*. Decisions such as that have resulted in "extremely close" relationships with both of his grown children, plus enormous vocational success. Dr. Dobson said, "You can do a lot of things to restore balance, but if it comes right down to it, you may have to get another job. That's what I did. I had to do something for my family" (*New Man,* May/June 2003, p. 19).

I have a dear friend with whom I was recently talking about his relationship with his father. He is one of the many people who have told me that their father practically never hugged them or told them, "I love you." My heart broke as he recounted how he never received his father's approval. Though his dad was a church-going man and a deacon in the Baptist church they attended, he never told my friend that he loved him. In effect, my friend rarely sought to build a relationship with his son, likely because his father had not sought to build a relationship with him. Years later, the result in my friend's life is a temptation to seek to earn the approval of his father by accomplishments. That tendency was even a temptation to carry over into his work and other relationships as well: I must earn the approval of other people.

I am blessed to have two older sisters. As we talk about our father, we all share the same sentiments about him. Dad had a way of making us feel close to him and special. We praise God that we did not feel a pressure to earn his approval. We lived in the reality of being people who already had his approval because we were his children. If there is a key to this closeness with Dad and the sense of approval we had from him, I think it is simply this: *Dad sought to build a relationship with his kids.*

I remember talking with a church member one day who was having some intense family problems. His marriage was shallow and unsatisfying. His daughter was abandoning many things she had been taught and was developing a rebellious attitude. As I was listening to his situation I asked him if he was making an effort to build a relationship and emotionally connect with his wife and daughter. His response to me was, "I am not good at that kind of stuff." I basically shared with him that his situation did not give him the luxury of copping out because he did not feel particularly skilled at relationship building.

Youth ministry professor Richard Ross talks about our relationship with our children being like a three-legged stool. The first leg of the stool stands for the things we teach our children. The second leg of the stool stands for the example we set for our children. Most Christian homes strive at least to make basic progress in the first two areas. As you know, a three-legged stool needs all three legs to be strong in order for it to stand. The last leg of the stool is referred to as a heart connection. It is the relationship we build with our children. If we impart truth and set an example but do not have a heart relationship with our children, they are not likely to embrace the truths they have seen and heard from us.

As I think about my relationship with my father, I am eager to strive to have all three legs of the stool passed on to my children. That last stool leg of heart connection seems to be the most lacking in our day. Here are a few ways my father built a relationship with me:

1) *He made me feel like he wanted to be around me.* This gave me a subtle push toward his heart from my earliest

memories. Later in life, this feeling that he wanted me around him freed me to seek his counsel and receive his words for me. I try to regularly look my boys in the eye and say, "Do you know how special you are? It is so great to be your dad."

2) *He asked me questions.* "How was your day?" "What did you and your friends do?" "Hey Cliff, what are you listening to?" Without sounding like he was prying, Dad knew how to get me to talk. That is a key to a strong relationship. His asking me questions helped me always believe that he cared what I was thinking, how my day went, and what was important to me. I have found that some of my children do not like to talk about the mundane parts of their day. So instead of saying, "How was school"? I usually ask, "What did you all play in recess or P.E. today?" Or, "Who did you sit by at lunch today?"

3) *He let me ask him questions.* As I mentioned, my dad was interruptible. Since he asked me questions, I in turn felt free to ask him questions. I liked to ask him things about what he did as a boy. I got the scoop on how he and Mom met and remembrances of his youth.

   I also liked to ask him deep questions about God. Sometimes my version of theological questions could get peculiar. One night I had a serious question that must have sounded strange to him. I got to thinking about it after I kissed Mom and Dad goodnight; I lay in my bed and tried to go to sleep. I would sometimes talk to the Lord. One night I decided to blow God a kiss. But I was not sure if it reached heaven. The next day I had to talk to Dad and I asked him, "Dad, how do I kiss

God goodnight?" Dad set me free. He told me that I did not have to worry about kissing the Lord. Knowing that I could ask him something as nutty as that gave me comfort.

Since I knew Dad wanted a relationship with me and that I could ask him questions, when I was engaged to be married I asked him some candid questions about sex. As I mentioned, he equipped me well with "the talk." Having been gratefully preserved as a virgin by the grace of God, I was not exactly sure how this "act of marriage" thing worked. Dad gave me some pointers, insights, and tips that would have caused most people to blush. It is a precious memory to me.

4) *He wisely used the power of touch.* I would not describe Dad as a big teddy bear or overtly "touchy" person. But he knew how to give his family needed physical touch. Hugs. Pats. Firm grips. Those were a normal part of my growing up and young adult years. I have heard some fathers say that they do not know how to be affectionate with their kids because their fathers were not affectionate with them. I have some simple advice: learn! It is not that hard.
   Dads—be wise and appropriate with your touch, but by all means, touch your children. They are waiting for your tender but powerful touch of love and acceptance.

5) *He was generous with affirmation.* [18] **There is one who speaks rashly, like a piercing sword; but the tongue of the wise [brings] healing.**

   (Proverbs 12:18). "I love you." "Great job, son." "I am

so proud of you." Those words were so common that I hardly noticed them. Those words make a young boy grow up strong. Dads—do not let your kids grow up remembering only the harsh, angry words you spewed on them. Let them know you love them by giving them many encouraging words.

6) *He laughed hard.* In a sermon of Dad's called "Christ and Cancer," he simply encouraged people to keep good humor when experiencing affliction. That kind of admonition can only come from people experiencing true pain and adversity. It sounds hollow for me to say, "Hey…if you have cancer, make sure you take time to laugh." But Dad said it powerfully and indeed lived it out. He regularly kept lighthearted until the very end. One of his colleagues shared that when the seminary professors would go to lunch, Dad would sometimes laugh so hard that he would be bent over and gasping for breath.

Family experts agree that laughing with your family is a key element to creating a lasting and authentic bond. I have a mind full of memories that involve our family laughing out loud. We would recall family stories or awkward moments and laugh hard. Seeing Dad get really amused was always a sight. He would bowl over and hold his stomach from laughing so hard.

Don't get me wrong. There were times when Dad aimed to be funny, but just wasn't. In other words, he had a stash of stale jokes that he used and reused. But neither he nor I minded. It was part of his charm. For instance, when we would visit his family, his mother would say to him at dinner, "Tommy, can I pass you the beans?" He would reply, "I'm sorry, Mother. I do not eat beans on Tuesday." She would never fail to laugh even after she had heard it dozens of times. My sisters would roll their eyes. I just figured that is what you say to your mom when you get older. But I like the fact that we never saw this PhD get too distinguished to laugh. We never saw this cancer patient get too sullen to chuckle.

7) *Play hard.* In addition to laughing hard, Dad was also big on playing hard. We went to Dallas Cowboys games, Dallas Mavericks games, and TCU football games (sorry non-Texas sports fans). I loved sports, but I never had tremendous success as a player myself. Nonetheless, my dad was at every one of my athletic events as a kid…even when I played in the church league in high school.

We went on some of the funniest city-boy camping trips. We went to a local state park. We set up the tent, and then went into town for McDonald's and a movie. We camped out, spent the night, and went fishing and paddle boating…then headed home.

Dad also took our family on simple, memorable trips. If we were at an amusement park, he would ride the big, frightening rides—not because he wanted to, per se, but because relationship was valuable to him.

We all love our children. But this particular lesson I am learning from my father pushes me to go beyond merely loving them. Do I know them? Am I building trust with them? Am I allowed into their private worlds? Do I have their hearts? We must keep such questions in mind as we seek to build relationships with our children.

Chapter 11

Be Honest

Did you hear about the father who was teaching his son different Bible verses about lying? He was concerned that his boy live a life of honesty. I love the answer that this little boy gave to his father when he asked him, "Son, what is a lie?"

The boy mixed up a couple of Bible verses and replied, "Father, a lie is an abomination to the Lord, but a very present help in time of need." All of us have felt like that in the past. We know that lying is wrong, but sometimes we are dishonest if we feel like it can help us through a tight spot.

Lying is wrong not merely because one of the Ten Commandments is [16] **Do not give false testimony against your neighbor.** (Exodus 20:16). Lying is wrong because deceit is abhorrent to the nature of God. Psalms 31:15 refers to the Lord as "the God of Truth." Hebrews 6:18 teaches that truthfulness is so foundational to the character and essence of God that "it is impossible for God to lie." God hates falsehood because it is so abhorrent to his truthful and righteous being. Scripture also says, "The Lord detests lying lips, but he delights in men who are truthful" (Proverbs 12:22).

On the other hand, Satan is referred to in Scripture as "the father of lies" in John 8:44. The native language of the evil one is deceitfulness. Therefore, when a Christian lies, he is cooperating with Satan. When a believer speaks the truth, he is cooperating with God.

A verse that has challenged me about honesty is, [23] **Buy—and do not sell—truth,wisdom, instruction, and understanding**(Proverbs 23:23). This is a verse I pray for my children. I ask God to make my five boys honest men who have the courage to do the right thing even when no one is looking. My passion to pray for my boys' honesty grew out of my father's example in truthfulness. He was not flashy about his integrity. He was subtle and contagious about it. He simply told the truth and expected the truth from me.

I was recently reading a letter that one of Dad's friends wrote to my mother when Dad died. The letter described Dad as the greatest example of a person of integrity that he ever knew. That description echoed exactly my own sentiments about Dad.

This reality made lying to him as a kid one of the last things on my "to-do" list. His love for the truth was such an essential part of who he was. That, coupled with the deep intentionality he had at pursuing a relationship with me, made me truly want to be honest. One of the worst memories of my childhood is when I took a pack of gum from a drugstore when I was five or six years old. This isolated incident was not so horrible for me because I knew that I had taken something that was not mine.

What I felt so badly about was that I emphatically lied to Dad when he questioned me about where I had gotten the gum. I begged the Lord to forgive me for that countless times. I know he did. But I experienced a short breach in my relationship with my father because I could not be honest with him.

Dad had a long talk with me one day about honesty when I was a boy. It happened because of a prayer request I gave in Sunday school. Some seminary students were teaching my fourth grade Sunday school class. They asked us kids if any of us had any prayer requests. I was getting flustered one week because a lot of kids had some really exciting prayer requests to lift up to the Lord. I did not want to miss out on the fun so I made up a prayer request. I said, "Pray for my family."

"Sure. Why, Cliff?" the teacher asked.

"My uncle died," I replied.

"Is that your father's or your mother's brother?" For some reason I told them my father's brother had died. I suppose I had forgotten that my dad was an only child.

My Sunday school teacher was a seminary student. He ran into Dad on the seminary campus and told Dad he was sorry to hear about the loss of his brother. Dad inquired as to where they heard such a thing. Let's just say that I got a stern "talking to" when Dad got home that day. I was caught red-handed in a senseless lie. I just thought it would be cool to share a prayer request. My dad made it clear how offensive lying was to a holy God. The Scripture is true when it says that "truthful lips endure forever, but a lying tongue lasts only a moment" (Proverbs 12:19).

Sometimes it is hard to be honest in the little things. Christ said that he who is dishonest with little, will be dishonest with much. You may have heard about the manager who was asked by his laziest employee for a recommendation for another job. The manager thought hard all night for something that would be honest without hurting the young man's chances. He finally wrote: "You will be lucky if you can get him to work for you." Sometimes we are put in situations where it is challenging to be forthright and honest. But the Bible teaches in Luke 16:10b that [10] **Whoever is faithful in very little is also faithful in** "

Some feel that we should simply recognize that everybody is dishonest to some degree and that lying is therefore a necessary part of our society. I could not disagree more with the thought that we should accept deceitfulness as part of life. I remember seeing my dad's honesty and integrity come into play when I was a college student. He was helping me buy a car during my senior year. We went to a car lot and picked out a used car. We took the car to a shop around the corner to a trusted mechanic named Chuck. Chuck looked under the hood. He asked Dad where he was buying the car from. When Dad told him the name of the car dealer, Chuck smiled and said, "I am good friends with the owner there." Chuck smiled and quickly called the owner's office and said, "I am here in my shop with Tommy Lea. Yeah. He is my uncle and I would like you all to give him a good deal."

My dad saw what was happening and became very uncomfortable. I stepped back and said to myself, "How is Dad going to handle this one?" When Chuck hung up the phone Dad said to him with a polite but serious tone, . "Chuck, that is not true.

I cannot receive a discount like that." Chuck dismissed it all and said it would be fine.

As soon as we went back to the car lot, our salesman said, "Well, well. You know the owner, huh? I am supposed to give you a great deal." Dad immediately said to the salesmen, "Look. I am not related to the man who called the owner. I did not ask him to do that. I am sorry that he did that." Dad's words came off awkwardly, but they meant the world to me. The man dismissed them…not really knowing what to say or do. But I never forgot them.

I learned that day that honesty is tough. I learned that sometimes honesty can cost you something—like money. Dad could have easily gone along with the story. No one would likely have ever known but me. But I also knew that Dad went home that night and put his head on his pillow in peace. Can you imagine what Dad would have felt if he had caved and gone along with the harmless lie? He might have saved about $1,000 or so, but he would not have had the peace of God in his heart. He also would have dismantled my understanding of truth…and tarnished his example to his devoted son.

Something else about Dad's honesty is that I don't recall broken promises given to me. I knew friends who had fathers who would constantly promise things to their children but would never deliver. "Hey son, I am going to come home early from work and throw the ball with you." Then yet another unfulfilled vow: "Next week we are going to the amusement park." When those promises were not kept, a great breach of trust occurred. Fathers often get into a panic because they feel guilty for not spending enough time with their children. So in an effort to "make it up to them," promises of doing something special are uttered. My dad's style was never to over-promise. As I look back on my childhood, Dad did not promise me many things. But whenever he did, you could take it to the bank. Though I didn't realize it, this made his credibility very high with me.

We have all been shocked and hurt by discovering that someone we admire proves to be dishonest. A great benefit to Dad's truthfulness was that he always came off as extremely trustworthy to me. If Dad told me something, I did not embark on a fact-checking mission to see if what he said was accurate. If we were in the car driving and he said something to me about cars, English, science, politics, entertainment, or anything under the sun, I did not question it because I knew Dad was emphatically honest. How did this help me as his son? When Dad told me that he loved me, I really believed it. When he told me that God loved me, I also devoutly believed it. The end result was that I got my esteem from how much he loved me and how much God loved me.

Men—if your words of affirmation are not sinking into your child's heart, it may be because they are not sure they can trust your words. Have you demonstrated dishonest character by disregarding rules, "stretching the truth," and telling "white lies"? Have you broken promises again and again? Don't expect them to believe you when you say that God loves them and that you love them. Ask God to help you grow in the area of honesty…and you will see a direct correlation to a stronger relationship with your child. Say with David, "[163] **I hate and abhor falsehood, [but] I love Your instruction.** (Psalms 119:163).

Chapter 12

Be Accepting

Paul said in Romans 15:7, **Therefore accept one another, just as the Messiah also accepted you, to the glory of God.** The word "accept" in this verse means "to receive with full welcome." Sometimes we think that being "accepting" is the same thing as being condoning. Condoning someone's sinful behavior or immoral lifestyle is to say, "It's no big deal that you behave that way." To be accepting of someone's sinful behavior is to say, "Though your behavior is wrong, I receive you as a person just like Christ will." Christ receives sinners in "full welcome" when they turn from sin and repent.

Christians in our day are not known for cultivating an attitude of acceptance of others. We are more prone to alienate others because of their behavior and to expect Christian behavior from non-Christians. Unfortunately, Christians in our day are more known for harsh, critical statements that repel the lost world.

The task of fatherhood demands this attitude of acceptance. Proverbs 22:15 states it well by saying, **Foolishness is tangled up in the heart of a youth**. Another way to say it is, "Kids do a lot of dumb things." We all did! Some things kids do are blatant rebellion. Other things are simply childish foolishness based on immaturity. So when a child does the obvious rebellious or foolish action, he or she is looking to how his or her parents will accept them. Will they forgive or hold a grudge? Will they correct or criticize? Will they act with compassion and mercy, or anger and rage? I would like to urge dads especially to be accepting.

Why do you think Paul singles out fathers in Ephesians 6:4 when he says, **fathers, don't stir up anger in your children** making it difficult for them to obey? I think it is partly because dads were universally considered the head of the home, but also because fathers are often quick to show retaliation and anger to a child's foolishness. To exasperate means to overcorrect and frustrate. God's Word is saying in essence, "Dads, while you train your child do not be a jerk and wound his or her spirit along the way. Correct and train with love!"

Many of us were appalled to hear of actor Alec Baldwin's "answering machine message" to his daughter. She is an adolescent girl who lives with her mother, Baldwin's estranged wife. He was angry with her about something and left a voicemail that was given to the press. On this voicemail, he expressed his anger and called her "a selfish little pig." While parenting mistakes of celebrities make front-page and top story news, the painful truth is that many fathers forfeit an attitude of acceptance in exchange for a "fault-finding" demeanor toward their children.

Though my dad was a man of great conviction and firm belief, he somehow maintained a beautiful balance of displaying an attitude of acceptance. This demeanor made people from all walks of life feel at home around my father. As a parent I am convinced that an attitude of acceptance is a vital trait for fathers. Our children are craving it.

I remember a few instances in my life where Dad's accepting heart shone especially brightly. One of them was when I was in the sixth grade. I had one of the strangest afternoons of my life. I was going on a Sunday afternoon bike ride with some friends in Fort Worth. I had ridden a few miles away from home on the ride. A guy in the group I was with saw a sign in front of a newly built home that said "Open House." The house was unfurnished, unfinished, unoccupied, and open. So he suggested we all go inside. It seemed okay since the sign did say "Open House." I assumed it was fine for folks to go inside and look at it. Our feet were muddy, so the concrete floor got a little messy. Within a few minutes of our being inside the house, a security guard came to the door and called us to him. He told us to wait by his car. Within another few minutes I saw four police cars pull up right beside us. *What is going on? Are those for us?* I wondered. Relieved that they did not slap the cuffs on us, the four of us quickly heeded our orders to get in the back seat of the police car.

I was experiencing something completely surreal. I was a goody-goody at best. My idea of getting in "trouble" was to be asked to spit my gum out in Sunday school. Now I was on my way to the "big house." I was driving down I-30 in Fort Worth desperately hoping I did not see anyone from church or the seminary. The officers said we were being accused of "vandalism." I was not sure what that word meant, but it did not sound good. I kept eerily quiet in the back seat the whole way home. While I worked hard to fight back tears, the officers took us to separate holding rooms. What I did not like at all about those rooms is that they had a doorknob on the entrance into the room…but did not have one from the inside. As far as I was concerned, I was in a cell. I deduced that this is where the "bad kids" hung out until they were taken to "kid jail."

As I waited in my "cell," my mind focused on one thing: *the reaction of my father*. "What on earth are my parents going to think? My Sunday afternoon bike ride has turned me into a criminal suspect. My life is over. It has been nice." I will truly never forget what happened next. The officer called me and asked me to follow him. I walked down a hallway and saw my father waiting for me. There was a beaming compassion in his eyes. Dad seemed relieved to see that I was fairly composed. He had to know I was dying inside. As I tried to speak and apologize and explain things, I was interrupted by a strong, long man hug. That was just what I needed! I did not expect him to yell at me, but neither did I think there would be such Christ-like mercy. I was accepted.

We certainly talked about my unwise choice that afternoon. I also learned my lesson by being grounded. But my trust and respect of Dad flourished that day.

I remember a similar response from Dad in a totally different situation. I was twenty-one years old. I was not known for getting inordinately "stressed out." That was my sister's job. But I don't know of any other way to describe how I felt one afternoon during my last semester of my senior year of college. I was totally worn out. I was engaged to be married, scheduled to graduate from college, about to start seminary, and feeling the burden of what it meant to be a real live grown-up. During my weekly call home, when Dad got on the phone to ask how I was doing, I completely broke down. I couldn't speak anymore. I just sobbed.

Since this was unusual for me, it was also awkward for me. At first Dad was concerned that there was something else besides inordinate pressure going on with me. When I could give him no clearly defined reason for my sorrow, he gave up trying to diagnose me. He simply waited, listened, supported, and probably hung up the phone and did some serious praying. I was much better within a few days. However, something that stayed with me is how my dad stuck by me and accepted me with full welcome even when I was showing some strange behavior.

My oldest son is a wonderful young man. Part of growth as an adolescent is learning to open up. His natural bent sometimes tends to bottle up things he is going through. I asked him recently, "Nate, if you were going through something really stressful or worrisome or troubling, would you come and talk to me?" He said, "Dad, I have never felt that way. I guess I would. I don't know." I just told him, "Nate, I realize you may not want to talk to me about stuff you are going through. But I am telling you now...I would love to listen and be there for you with whatever you are going through."

I felt that way from my father. Therefore, it led me to open up and go deep with him. For instance, as I mentioned previously, my dad was good about keeping me informed about sexual issues. But when I was engaged and had just a few weeks before my marriage, I was ready for a slightly deeper version of "the talk." It was almost "game time." I had to know just a little more. I was finished with college. I was about to get married and start seminary. I was home. Dad and I were outside doing some yard work. I said to him, "Well, Dad, I am looking forward to my honeymoon." He took my bait, and we launched into unforgettable conversation about the joys of marital intimacy…complete with some "how-to" tips.

I do not know many dads who would be that comfortable with a conversation like that. I also do not know many sons who would bring it up for fear of their father's reaction. I think I was freed up to talk that way because Dad gave me his blessing of acceptance.

Dad's acceptances of me made me realize that I could make a mistake and do something stupid, yet still know that I was loved. Our homes desperately need to create an atmosphere of "mistakes are not encouraged, but are allowed."

Chapter 13

Love the Lost

When my dad was a pastor in Birmingham, Alabama, I was a young child. I remember going to some homes with him on church visitation. Our church was in a transitioning neighborhood. Dad began teaching the people how to share their faith through the burgeoning "Evangelism Explosion" program. Week after week, Dad would send out teams to ask people, "If you were to die today, do you know for certain where you would spend eternity?" This method helped Dad for years to come. It also promoted a true concern for the souls of people who did not have a personal relationship with Christ.

Dad told me a story about making sure that we came across as truly caring for people rather than merely getting through our presentation. As he was training people in "Evangelism Explosion," there was an admirable senior adult lady in his group. She went out on Dad's team in the neighborhood one evening. Dad asked her if she would go through the memorized plan of salvation that was taught in the course. The people listening to the presentation stopped the lady and asked her a question. In an irritated tone they asked, "Where did you learn that?" The question embarrassed the lady and Dad.

The point Dad shared with me about that story is to avoid sharing your faith in a way that sounds like a memorized, canned, sales presentation. Share the gospel with concern, care, and sensitivity to people. Look them in the eye. Pause for questions. Exude the love of Christ. Treat them as real people with real questions and situations.

In addition to being involved in such direct approaches to sharing the gospel, I also noticed Dad out building relationships and talking to our neighbors. In Alabama, and later when we moved to Texas when I was eight, we were surrounded by people who barely went to church or did not go at all. He was intentional about being friendly and loving. By being a friend, God provided open doors to talk to people and demonstrate the love of Christ to the lost. These opportunities did not always end in someone giving his or her life to Christ. There was a couple down the street that had a son my age. When they learned that a "preacher" moved into the neighborhood and that his son would be playing with theirs, they openly told my dad to make sure not to proselytize his son. That did not keep my parents from building a relationship and demonstrating God's love to them. That relationship my father developed opened the door for me to share the gospel in detail with their son later in high school and college. Though he was resistant, a seed of the gospel was planted that I pray God will bring to fruition in his time.

That was a great example to me as I moved into my first home. There was a neighbor named J.C. who lived across the street. We often exchanged smiles and greetings, but had not had occasion to really get to know each other. My initial impression of J.C. was that he did not know Christ. I began praying for him. In those days, I was active in sharing my faith, but not very inclined to build a friendship with someone unless he or she was a Christian. He often stayed outside and worked on his truck. There were many times when I was about to go over and "give him the gospel" and invite him to church. But it seemed that almost every time I was heading over to talk to him, either I got a phone call or he had gone inside.

One day I finally got a chance to go over and have a long talk with him. I began to ask him questions about himself. When he shared about a painful divorce he had gone through, I asked him, "What did that experience do to the way you view God"? To my surprise, J.C. opened wide up. It led me to share of my experience of receiving Christ. As we were winding down our conversation, he looked at me and said, "One thing I appreciate about you is that after all these months you have lived here, you have never tried to preach to me and invite me to your church." I gulped and thanked God that he had postponed my encounter to share Christ with him until that moment—and not a moment too soon. Ever since my experience with J.C., I have sought to be obedient when the Lord leads me to share the gospel with someone I do not know, while being willing to share Christ through building a relationship as well.

Missions were always an important part of Dad's life. He told me that when he first sensed a call to ministry, he sought

God's will about becoming an international missionary. Though God never called him in that direction, Dad was involved in traveling overseas to do short-term missions throughout his ministry.

Something that encouraged me is that his several-year battle with cancer did not extinguish his concern for the lost. There seemed to be an increase in a love for the lost and tenderness toward missions in his later years. He and Mother went on some wonderful international mission trips in his latter years to Eastern Europe, Africa, and Asia to encourage missionaries and share the gospel.

Another situation that showed that Dad's love for the lost was increasing as he battled cancer involved how he related to my sister Marcie in her call to missions. There is some background to her call to missions that involved Dad and me praying for the same part of the world. In the early 1990s, there was an international relief crisis in the Horn of Africa. Help and relief were needed in the strong Islamic region. As I received more information about what was going on there, I began to pray that God would save people from that region. I also prayed Matthew 9:38 for that region, asking the Lord to "send out workers" to the fields and prepare many workers to go and share his amazing love.

Unbeknownst to me, my father was praying the same thing for that region. God had simply burdened his heart to lift up that region of the world. Neither of us knew that as we prayed, my sister and her new husband were also praying about God's plan for their lives, and they began talking with the mission board about serving in this dark area—the Horn of Africa.

My sister and brother-in-law went to serve there for a two-year assignment. They had a challenging and adventurous two years. As they came back, they sensed God calling them back to that region for a career assignment. When they were leaving, Dad had been diagnosed with a serious and aggressive form of cancer. Marcie was close to her father. She wanted to be with him in case Dad was not going to make it.

Being the gentle and loving leader he was, Dad called a "family meeting" to discuss Marcie's pending departure to the mission field for a long-term assignment. I will never forget that day. Marcie, her husband Alan, my sister Lisa, and I sat in our family living room with Mom and Dad. Dad wanted us to know that though he had cancer and had no guarantees on the length of his life, he fully supported Marcie and Alan and their decision to move across the world to share the gospel of Christ. It was the most beautiful release of his daughter to the will of God. He was in essence saying, "The lost are more important than family dinners at Thanksgiving. Yes I have cancer, but my daughter is answering God's call to serve among those who have never heard the gospel, and I am delighted about it."

I also have a vivid memory of Dad's concern for lost people during the last few weeks of his life in a Fort Worth hospital. He came to know the nurses who were caring for him. Dad's graciousness amid his pain and agony continued to exude from his life. There was one particular male nurse from Vietnam that Dad had gotten to know. I was in the room one day when they talked. Dad began bringing up the Lord and how important it was for everyone to have a relationship with Christ. The man spoke back and said, "I don't really believe in that." Dad spoke with a sober politeness and looked at him and said, "You are taking a great risk if you are wrong." The man was not offended, but didn't know what to say. He fairly quickly left the room. But I was taught a valuable lesson about caring for the souls of others even when I am consumed with my own pain. Dad's example drives me to pray that God will always give to me his heart for the lost...regardless of what physical limitations I may encounter.

Paul was under house arrest when he wrote the book of Colossians. He asked the church at Colossae to pray for him. If I were thrown in jail for preaching the gospel and wrote a note to my church, it would probably read something like, "Get me some awesome lawyers and get me out of here now!" Instead of being consumed by his vexing situation, Paul asked the church to **...pray also for us that God may open a door to us for the message, to speak the mystery of the Messiah** (Colossians 4:3).

Rather than succumb to our schedules, trials, and fears, we should strive to follow Paul's example and love the lost.

Chapter 14

Trust God

When I began my first year of college in 1988, I read a life-changing book by Jerry Bridges called *Trusting God.* During that first semester I was going through homesickness, career decisions, and adjusting to life in a new place without my family. The premise of that book was that since the Bible teaches God is wise, good, and sovereign, he can be trusted at all times. Therefore, worry, fear, and anxiety should not be a part of the Christian life. I wish I could say that I mastered the application of those concepts during my freshmen year of college. However, I have leaned on the truths from that book all these years and have imperfectly sought to make progress in trusting God.

As I reflect on my dad's life further, I see that trusting God was a vital part of his daily life. I honestly have no memories of him caving into worry, anxiety, and fear. Surely he had moments of these things behind closed doors or in his prayer times. I do not mean that there was an absence of stress. Simply raising me was certainly plenty of stress. But I remember Dad living life with a sense of God's peace. Isaiah 26:3 says of the Lord, "[3] **You will keep in perfect peace the mind [that is] dependent [on You], for it is trusting in You.**

For instance, for most families one of the biggest challenges to trust God is in the area of personal finances. Dad had this compelling balance when it came to money. He was diligent in giving and was a great example in saving. But he also managed to provide essentials and some extras for our family without being overwhelmed at the task or making us feel as if he were frustrated or broke. I have friends who tell me that anytime they asked their parents for things, they responded by saying, "We do not have any money." Though we were definitely denied some "wants," Dad never said anything like, "I am a simple preacher. Do not ask for anything expensive this Christmas." As I seek to practice God's principles of managing money and provide for my own family, there are definitely times I feel a temptation toward anxiety. I strive to make prayer the first reaction to this temptation. I am also blessed by remembering Dad's strong and peaceful attitude about daily issues like money.

Dad also showed he trusted God when we would have setbacks as a family. One important issue for our family growing up was the eyesight of my oldest sister Lisa. She developed a tragic loss of retina in her eye that made her legally blind. Lisa's loss of eyesight understandably broke my mother's heart. Though Mom usually kept it together well, I distinctly remember Mom breaking down with large sobs one day in our living room because Lisa's driver's license was suspended due to her vision.

As Dad would talk to us about Lisa's vision, it was like a shepherd calmly walking among the sheep. He talked about some new glasses they were going to buy to help Lisa drive again. He and Mom sacrificially took care of her and sought to get her the finest help she could have. I do not remember everything going on during that time, but my memories of Dad are filled with someone who was confidently looking to God to help his daughter. Rather than succumbing to fear of the unknown about his child's future, he banked his trust in God. Dad's example helped me deal with fear when Luke, my second born son, had a few unexplained seizures a few years ago. Though he has gotten proper treatment, and God has kept his seizures from returning, it was definitely a journey of faith for me initially.

Trusting God for the less significant daily cares is what prepares us to trust him during the truly tragic events of life. In an article about his cancer in 1998, Dad said, "I have renewed the conviction that God is sovereignly in charge, even in my sickness. He has not left me. He is concerned about my spiritual good." That is simply stated but profound to me. We are tempted to be like Job's wife and simply curse God and die when tragedy comes our way (Job 2:9). But Dad had the spirit of Job about his cancer. **Should we accept only good from God and not adversity?"** " (Job 2:10). Trust comes when we believe God remains in charge regardless of circumstances.

A clip from a sermon Dad preached a few months before his death illustrates the kind of faith Dad was pursuing in his own life:

> I don't protest or complain about the justice of what's in my life now. I thank God that he has given me his grace, he's let me do things that I never dreamed I'd be able to do. He's given me blessings for which I could never thank him. I've been here nearly four years with cancer. I thank God that I'm able after four years to preach and to effectively serve him. You see life isn't fair. Thank God there's grace, and as we come to know God, we come better to understand that grace and to thank him for it.

Trust in God reaches a higher plane when we view our trials as a fresh opportunity to get to know the Lord. Dad said that he began to view cancer as an opportunity to know God more deeply and to experience his grace. He often said his favorite Scripture passage was Lamentations 3:22–23: **Because of] the LORD's faithful love we do not perish, for His mercies never end.**[23] **They are new every morning; great is Your faithfulness!** (B)

He once said to me, "I rest in that verse." Do we rest in God's promises when we experience deep pain? Bank your hope on the faithfulness of God amidst deep pain and you will experience God new every morning.

I received a letter from one of my dad's former students, Dr. John Redmond, in September of 2006. He is now an associate pastor at a church in Pasadena, Texas. We had never met, but he had been thinking about Dad and wanted to convey to me how much my father meant to him. Here is a quote from his letter that illustrates this point of trusting God:

> *I just want you to know that your father was a tremendous blessing to my life. I had him for New Testament and for the book of Revelation. At the time I had him for the class on Revelation, he was battling his cancer. I will never forget his faith in God and his faithfulness to God's work. It was interesting, when I had your dad for New Testament, he taught us about the grace of God. When I had him for the book of Revelation, he demonstrated the grace of God by trusting in him at a very difficult time.*

John later elaborated to me about Dad's impact on his life. He recounted that one day during the Revelation class, Dad had to immediately go to the hospital for a procedure after class. He explained to the class that he brought a suitcase with him so that he could head straight to his car and make it in time for his treatment. (That is so Dad. Mr. Prepared!) John says that Dad lectured effortlessly and powerfully on the book of Revelation for an hour and a half as if he did not have a care in the world. At the end of class, he asked the class to pray for him for his upcoming treatment at MD Anderson Hospital in Houston. Then he grabbed his suitcase and headed out the door. John shared that Dad exuded a powerful sense of peace throughout the class period. That made a lasting point on many in the room about the importance of trusting God through pain and trials.

The Bible says, [26] **In the fear of the LORD one has strong confidence and his children have a refuge.** (Proverbs 14:26). The truth is that life is hard. Christ told us in John 16:33 that in this world you will have tribulation all around. Though my life is far from tragic compared to many, when I experience the trials of life I still sense the refuge of the secure fortress that came from my dad's trust in God. I long for my children to taste the sweetness of this refuge by being a father that trusts God in all things.

Something that strengthens our trust in God is a conviction of his faithfulness. 2 Timothy 2:13 says, [13] if we are faithless, He remains faithful, for He cannot deny Himself In Dad's commentary on the Pastoral Epistles he says, "Human faithlessness only serves to decorate the faithfulness of God" (New American Commentary on 1, 2 Timothy, Titus, page 211). In other words, God is faithful and trustworthy even when we give up. There is nothing in us and no force on earth that can penetrate, change, or shake the faithfulness of our almighty God.

Getting gravely ill and leaving your new grandchildren, the wife you deeply love, and the work you enjoy before age sixty in our day is tragic. I never saw Dad be worried and anxious or despondent about such a terrible thing that was happening to him. Though he would have definitely preferred to keep serving the Lord and grow old with his bride, he had firmly decided that God knew what he was doing. He reminds me of the man that David described in Psalms 112:6–7. [6] **He will never be shaken. The righteous will be remembered forever.**[7] **He will not fear bad news; his heart is confident, trusting in the LORD.**

I cannot shake the powerful example he left me of steadfast confidence in God.

Chapter 15

Be Authentic

There is a haunting statement about the Pharisees in Matthew 23:5. Christ says of the self-righteous religious leaders of the day, [5] **They do everything** [a] **to be observed by others** "Everything they do is for men to see." Christ also described them as hypocrites, whitewashed tombs, and filthy on the inside in this dark passage. I have always wanted to take Matthew 23 to be a reminder to live an authentic and genuine Christian life. I do not want a faith that is marked by vain ambition, heartlessness toward others, and living trapped by the opinions and estimations of others.

I got a note recently from one of Dad's former students that said, "Your father is one of my heroes. I had him for New Testament at SWBTS. I'll never forget the walk across campus that I shared with him on the way to class one day. It was not long after he was diagnosed with cancer. I told him that I was praying for him. I can still see his face as he expressed his appreciation—his sincerity really touched my heart."

Recently I was asking my wife Suzy what she remembers most about Dad. The first thing that came out of her mouth was that he was real and genuine. Frankly, I think Suzy was intimidated when she first met him. Since we attended the same university, Suzy had met Dad briefly on campus before. But I remember as we drove to my house when Suzy first came home as "my girlfriend," I talked about my parents with glowing detail. The impression she had about Dad was that he was a larger than life, brilliant scholar.

But when Dad hugged and greeted her and began peppering her with personal questions, she instantly was put at ease. Suzy went on to tell me, "I knew he was deeply intelligent, but I appreciate that he never made me feel stupid."

Dad and Mom continued to put Suzy at ease by wholeheartedly welcoming her into the family. I loved watching how they genuinely loved and accepted her. I remember one Saturday morning Dad called me up. Suzy and I had been married just a little more than a year. I answered the phone and Dad asked to speak with Suzy. I thought it was a bit odd that we did not talk. He and Suzy talked for a few minutes, and then she hung up the phone smiling. "What was that about, Suz?"

She went on to tell me that Dad just called her to express how grateful he was that I got to marry her. He had been thinking about how blessed our family was to have her as a daughter-in-law and just wanted to call and convey that to her. That was certainly not the heart of someone with mixed motives, but a genuine heart moved by love for others.

Another factor in Dad's authentic demeanor was his slowness to talk about himself. I remember as a boy my mother told me that Dad was writing a book. When his first commentary came out in the early 1980s, I thought it was the coolest thing in the world. As the opportunity to write other theological books and biblical commentaries increased, I remember going to Christian bookstores and trying to find his books on the shelf. I recall telling Dad what a great opportunity it was to write books. My memory is that he was quite reserved to celebrate those accomplishments with me. He always seemed quite unimpressed with himself. Dad also got the opportunity to preach at some large churches, such as Second Baptist Houston. I kept trying to pump him for information about what Dr. Ed Young's office was like. Dad took those things in stride and let me know by example that "to live is Christ." He had what Paul described in 2 Corinthians 11:3 as **a complete and pure**[a] **devotion to Christ.** He was not interested in a big career break. He wanted to serve the Lord and preach God's Word. Whatever blessings God decided to give him in that venture were up to God.

Something else that made Dad come across as genuine was his ability to talk about a variety of subjects. It is true that as believers our whole lives should be about Christ, and that everything we do is to intentionally be done for God's glory. I still think that means that one can have a biblical perspective of entertainment, politics, sports, and issues of the day. Although I treasure the times I asked Dad the deep biblical and theological questions, I also loved hearing why he liked Ronald Reagan instead of Jimmy Carter. I appreciated him making me sit still to watch *Chariots of Fire*. I liked when he stopped in the hallway when my sister's radio was blasting Kool and the Gang's hit song, "Celebration." My dad listened to the chorus where it says, "Celebrate good times. C'mon." He turned to me and said, "I like that song." He was getting dangerously close to sounding "cool" to me.

It was Dad who taught me why the sanctity of life and the death penalty were not mere political issues, but biblical issues that were being made to appear only political. We also talked about civil rights and racism, Civil War history, cults, old age, the NBA, money management, and manners. The fact that Dad could keep his commitment to Christ and then talk about a variety of subjects and jump and holler when the Dallas Cowboys scored was a blessing to me.

One thing Dad did not get to do nearly as long as he desired was grandparent. My oldest son was the first grandchild. He was a mere five years old when Dad passed. There were four other grandchildren under five when Dad died. My brief glimpse of Dad as a grandparent was a beautiful sight. That was one of the ways he seemed most authentic to me. When my son Luke was about three years old, Dad wrote this letter to Luke:

Dear Luke,

I am glad that you are coming to visit Paw Paw in several weeks. I enjoy seeing you when you can come. I also enjoy talking with you on the telephone. I can tell that you are growing big and strong, and I am happy for the chance to see you when you can come to Ft. Worth.

You have enjoyed playing in our backyard where we can see the many dogs around our house. I hope that you can use our sliding board and that you can go with me to the duck park and see some of the ducks there.

When your dad was a little boy, he enjoyed camping outdoors under the stars. I liked to take him with me, cook his supper over a fire, and listen for the noise at night as we tried to sleep. We heard birds and crickets. We also could hear dogs barking. I hope one of these days to take you camping outdoors. I think you will like it.

Much love,
Paw Paw

This did not sound like an over-dignified PhD in theology. He was into kids and playing! I grinned from ear to ear as I read this note the first time. I wanted to always maintain the kind of authenticity to play with kids and meet them at their level.

Chapter 16

Die Well

"Cliff, you had the privilege of knowing for certain that your father was an ***excellent*** *man."*

Those words rested on me with a piercing sweetness as I stood in a greeting line at the funeral home in early July of 1999. That is what the late Bible professor, Dr. Curtis Vaughn, said to me on the day I hoped would never come. It was the day after my father lost his battle with cancer at the age of sixty. Dr Vaughn's words were so simple. Yet he meant them deeply. Hearing them was a great step in what would be an intense personal battle with grief.

I still think about those words on a regular basis. God gave me an "excellent man" as father. As I think of those words, I quickly hear the words of Christ ringing to me, **Much will be required of everyone who has been given much.** " (Luke 12:48).

What was involved in Dad's being an "excellent man"? There are many factors involved. But a significant factor was how Dad died. Another colleague of Dad's, Dr. Tommy Briscoe, came up to me at Dad's funeral and said, "Tommy taught us how to live, and he taught us how to die." I think that we are missing in our day an intentional focus on learning how to die.

My dad's pastor was Dr. Michael Dean, from Travis Avenue Baptist Church in Fort Worth. I had the privilege of working on Dr. Dean's staff for a few years and enjoyed hearing him talk of my father. One day as we were talking about Dad, he said to me, "Your father died with such dignity." Dr. Dean recalled helping my father three weeks before his death. My parents were coming home from the Southern Baptist Convention in New Orleans. They left early because my father began to feel bad. Dr. Dean and his wife Nan came home on the same flight as my parents. He took delight in helping my parents in and out of the airport. He could see that my dad's strength was fading. However, he saw the power of God's peace at work in him through physical pain. There was not an alarming self-centeredness about a man and his disease. There was the serene dignity of one whose heart rested in God.

My dad learned a lot about how he wanted to die from watching his mother die. In the mid-1980s, his mother began her battle with cancer. We all called her "Les" (short for Mary Leslie). Les was a kind and gracious woman, but as previously mentioned, she was not known for being emotionally stable. She was raised in a traditional home complete with prejudice and a nominal faith. She was afraid of black people all her life. She would even recount to us as grandchildren how she was afraid that blacks would hurt her. She worried constantly. She put undue pressure on my father to keep in closer contact with her.

She ultimately died in 1989 from ovarian cancer. After one of Dad's visits with her, I remember Dad warning me about some things he observed. Her fears, worries, and prejudices were accentuated as she struggled with and faced death. She became harder to relate to and more difficult to be around. Essentially, her worst came out as she died. Years of what she had stored inside her heart were now bubbling over the surface of her heart.

What Dad warned me about was this: "Cliff, as you become aware of things in your life that God wants you to change, do not put them off. Seek God's help on overcoming them now." Dad was in his late forties when she was dying. It truly seemed like God was using her to inspire him to continue to strive to be emotionally and spiritually healthy all of his remaining days, a lesson that he would surely put into practice.

Dad got cancer some ten years after his mother. His experience with the dreaded disease played out much differently than hers. They both ended fatally. But it seems as though the more ill he became, the more Christ-like character came oozing out of his life. For years Dad had stored up countless Bible verses, hours of prayer, and rich theological works inside his heart. Now they were coming out. I remember writing my dad an e-mail during the year he died. I quoted Proverbs 18:14 that says, [14] **A man's spirit can endure sickness** and I told him how I saw Christ alive in him during his illness. I recall Mom sharing with me that my note had touched Dad. I was learning up close a vital truth about dying that I desperately wanted to remember my whole life.

One reason I know God used those experiences with his mother in Dad's life is because I never saw him be negative, anxious, or fearful in the years he battled cancer. He likely struggled with those feelings in the depths of his heart, but Dad continued to exude peace, joy, hope, rich confidence in God, and a true desire for God's glory.

I still remember him telling me that he had cancer. I was in my mid-twenties. He sat me down and told me about his unfortunate health report. He then immediately diverted to talk about how good it is that they detected his cancer early, how positive the research for prostate cancer has been lately, and the high chance of his cancer going into remission. He also told me that he trusted God to do whatever was best with him. He assured me that he would be praying for his own healing and asked me to do the same. All these words were spoken by a man at peace, a man ready to die and be with his Lord if needed.

Something else that blesses me when I think about the way Dad died is that he kept busy serving Jesus. After teaching New Testament at the seminary for sixteen years, in 1995 he was asked to become the dean of the School of Theology. He had just been diagnosed with cancer. He was honest with the school's leadership about his condition. Yet they insisted on his considering the job. After much prayer, he embarked on the huge task of leading the School of Theology for the world's largest seminary. In addition to this, he continued to travel and speak in churches on the weekend. He often was the interim pastor for churches who were looking for a pastor. He also was a busy writer during these days. He wrote a commentary on the books of Hebrews and James, as well as many Sunday school lessons for Lifeway Christian Resources. As a matter of fact, when he and Mom would check into a hotel room in Houston, before they would go to MD Anderson Hospital, Dad would bring his laptop and churn out Sunday school lessons that would be taught in thousands of churches around the country. He just stayed busy serving the Lord as long as his health would allow.

I remember as my father's health waned, I had some older colleagues in ministry advise me to go and spend as much time with my dad as I could. Though we saw each other regularly, we did not drive to their home every other weekend. The main reason was that Mom and Dad were out serving the Lord. Another reason I did not feel that I had to be with Dad constantly during his final days is because he and I had said everything we needed to say. It was joy that there was nothing else to say. As far as I could tell, there was nothing my father needed to say to anyone. His life was filled with a drive to serve the Lord and with relationships that were whole and not left unfinished.

I remember going to Dad's grave for the first time a few months after he had gone to be with the Lord. My mother, my wife, and my three children (at that time) went with me. My parents had bought plots together a few years before Dad died. His tombstone had his name and the years of his life marked on it. Right next to it was another tombstone bearing my mom's name and the date of her birth. There was a dash next to her birth date, but obviously no date for her death yet. My boys were asking whose grave that was. I told them it was "Papa's."

"Where is he?" they asked.

"Well, his body is in this grave under the ground. But Papa's heart and new body are up in heaven with the Lord Jesus," I said. They were taking it all in. They turned and pointed to my mother's grave. They asked whose that was. I told them that was where Nana's body was going to be buried. They looked at me and said, "When is she going in there?" I must have laughed and cried at the same time.

The truth is that none of us knows when we are going to face death. How and when will we die? Will we die well by honoring the Lord all our days? Something else I noticed on Dad's gravestone other than his name and dates of birth and death was an engraving of a Bible with the quote from Jesus in John 17:17. The quotation simply read, "Thy word is truth." What a powerfully succinct summary of Dad's life! He was a man who loved, treasured, and sought to live out God's Word up until his death. He had banked his whole livelihood and entire adult life on the fact that God has revealed himself in his Word and that his Word is absolute truth. It made me wonder if my life could possibly be summed up with such concise beauty.

At thirty-seven years old, unless Christ comes, I hope the Lord allows me to live so I can serve him and raise my dear family. Yet, when my time comes to go be with Jesus, I know how I want to die. I want to die longing for Jesus, serving him, and loving others with no regret. The first words I said as I preached my father's funeral sermon were a quote from Proverbs 10:7 that said: "[7] **The remembrance of the righteous is a blessing, but the name of the wicked will rot.**

I praise God that he empowered my father to die well, and his memory remains a tremendous blessing.

Chapter 17

Live for God's Glory

In the winter of 1995, I came to support my parents during Dad's first surgery to remove the cancer on his prostate. We had a wonderful visit. He shared something with me the night before the surgery that I will always remember.

He was sitting in his chair and he said, "Son, I want to show you a verse that the Lord has given me about the cancer." He then read to me from Philippians 1:20, which says, [20] **My eager expectation and hope is that I will not be ashamed about anything, but that now as always, with all boldness, Christ will be highly honored in my body, whether by life or by death.** He rarely preached to me at home as a kid, but I was eating up every word of this sermon from his living room recliner.

Dad went on to say to me, "I am praying this verse for myself. I want God to heal me. But the main thing I want is for

God to be exalted in my body. If that means my living, praise be to him. If it means my dying, may he be glorified."

I hated yet loved hearing those words. I was certainly not ready to lose my hero. I dreaded the thought of his leaving this world. But my huge respect of Dad, once again, skyrocketed that night. I said to the Lord, "I want to live like that, oh God. I want to be first and foremost concerned about your name and reputation." Dad's purpose was already clear in life. He wanted Christ to be lifted up "whether by life or by death." His passionate aim was to live for the glory of God. He preferred for that to be done while he was alive. But his ultimate concern was not *how* God would be glorified in him. He was simply concerned *that* God would be glorified in him.

I learned something powerful about parenting that day. It is this: your children are watching what is valuable to you by the way you suffer. Dad was going where many before him have gone. When faced with the strong possibility of death, early on his thoughts were moving toward the glory of God. I stayed close to him during his illness. Although he preferred to stay and grow old with his wife, kids, and grandchildren, his heart longed for God's will to be done and God's glory to be furthered.

Many fail to glorify God during their suffering because they are preoccupied with the concept of fairness. "It's not fair that I have cancer," some might utter. Dad was not concerned about fairness. Below is an excerpt from a sermon he delivered at Harvest Baptist Church in Watauga, Texas, in the spring of 1998:

One of the things that unfortunately you and I can get into saying when we have a disease like cancer is, "It isn't fair. God, I've served you, I've tried to live for you, and here I am coming down with cancer. I was trying to devote my life to you; it's not fair, it isn't right." And in the midst of protesting inwardly that things aren't fair I just want to say it to you this way: life isn't fair; it really isn't. Sometimes the wicked do seem to prosper and those who do seek to serve the Lord don't seem to prosper. There are things about life that really aren't fair. But I want to say that I am grateful for that because if life were exactly fair, then we would all get exactly what we deserve. My friend, if we got exactly what we deserve then the outlook for us would not be heaven but hell. I'd rather take my chances with grace than get what I deserve.

I do admit that life is not fair, but if life were completely fair, then God would dole out to us what we deserve. My friend, we don't deserve the mercy that God makes available, but he gives it. To those of us who recognize that life isn't fair, we can come to God and say to God, "I need your grace. I don't deserve to be doing what I am doing; I don't deserve the wife and children that God has given to me; these are acts of his grace."

God's glory—not resolving the issue of fairness—should be our focus. Zephaniah 3:5 says [5] **...morning by morning; He does not fail at dawn.**, In other words, though we may not see his fairness, God's judgments are wise and right every single day.

It was not as though Dad merely waited until his life was almost over to have this focus. He was intent about glorifying God throughout his life. Comments I heard from students and colleagues about his life were that Dad seemed to be free from ego-driven pride. There is an immaturity about many men in that they have a tendency to talk about their success and accomplishments. I liked hearing about Dad's next book or at what churches he was asked to speak. But he would never offer that information to me without my prodding. Neither would he talk long nor glowingly about it once I asked. Dad seemed to feel like the apostle Paul in 1 Corinthians 4:7, **What do you have that you didn't receive?** Since Dad was a recipient of God's grace, he seemed to have no use for boastful self-promotion.

We all battle with selfishness and pride. When I first started preaching, I was concerned that I was preaching for the compliments of people rather than for the sole pleasure of God. Everyone wants to hear how God is using you. But I began to see that I was developing a spirit of pride about my ministry. I asked Dad for some advice on how to battle pride and selfish ambition in ministry. He simply told me, "You can't make both God and yourself look good…" The point was clear: Focus on promoting God and his attributes—not yours. He alone is worthy. Truly Proverbs is right when it says, [18] **Pride comes before destruction,and an arrogant spirit before a fall.** (Proverbs 16:18).

Dad was quick to give others credit. When I was in high school, I once gave a ten-minute sermon at our church on "youth night." One of our church members was a colleague of Dad's. He came up to Dad and me one day and said to Dad, "Tommy, how does it feel to be the second best preacher in the family?" Dad said that he agreed with him and that nothing would make him happier.

They were certainly being gracious and light-hearted. But Dad was serious about giving others credit and living for the glory of God. He lived out the principle in 1 Corinthians 10:31, [31] **Therefore, whether you eat or drink, or whatever you do, do everything for God's glory.** "

Chapter 18

A Closing Challenge to Men

Recently my youngest son, Stephen, was showing Suzy and me an assignment that he did from his kindergarten class. The kids were to draw a picture of what they want to be when they grow up. Several of the girls in the class picked a teacher. Several of the boys drew pictures of athletes, policemen, and firemen. When Stephen was showing me the picture of what he wants to be when he grows up, I saw that he drew a picture of a dad. He also drew a picture of an extremely muscular and fit (surely not me) guy that looked like the king of the world. I got the impression that Stephen thinks that the job of being a dad is a career job. When given the chance to list what he wants to do for a living when he is a grown-up, he said, "Dad."

It touched me to see what kind of value Stephen has on his father. It seemed like a "profession" that he wanted to go into when he grew up. What about those us who are fathers right now? Do we view our role as father with such primacy and importance? Are we able to say with Solomon, *"My son, give me your heart"* (Proverbs 23:26).

As I close my reflections of the lessons I am still learning from my father, I am reminded of an apartment complex I visited several years ago in Fort Worth, Texas. The church where I was serving sought to do some outreach ministry in a needy neighborhood. I was talking to a representative of the apartment complex where we were considering doing an apartment ministry as he described all of the trouble with strife, drugs, and crime present at the complex. I asked for more information about the families that lived there. He said that out of the four hundred units to the apartment complex, there were only two units that had fathers living there. He elaborated to say there were plenty of men who were around—but the men came late at night and left early in the morning. Many children were fathered by these men, but these men had almost no involvement with these children.

If you were to drive to a nice suburban neighborhood, you might likely get very different statistics about how many fathers live at home with their families. But I would venture to say that in those nice homes the numbers of fathers that are actively engaged in building a relationship of love and trust with their children are few as well.

I sometimes throw my hands up in the air and ask, "Where are the men in our day?" Many men are like the fathers who have children in that apartment complex who have abandoned their families. Countless other men may share an address with their wife and children but essentially are absentee husbands and fathers. Sometimes it is because of work that men check out. But all too often, it is apathy, indifference, and cold neglect that cause men to be on the shelf in terms of leading their families.

I love the story of Abraham in the Old Testament. He was a man of both faith and frailty. Yet through all his ups and downs spiritually, I love the legacy of fatherhood that Abraham was called into. In Genesis 18:19, the Lord says of Abraham,[19] **For I have chosen him so that he will command his children and his house after him to keep the way of the LORD by doing what is right and just. This is how the LORD will fulfill to Abraham what He promised him."** God was saying in essence, "I have promised to bless Abraham and make him the father of many nations. That blessing will come to him as he directs his children and his household in my ways."

God was saying that Abraham was 100 percent responsible to lead his family. HE was to direct his children. He was not to be a grumpy, aloof, distant dad who would come home and bark out orders and keep everyone at bay. He was to be in the game with the children God entrusted to him. Men, so are we.

I realize that I am not prone to see my dad's weaknesses. Therefore I was not inclined to mention many in this book. Surely he was far more fragile and weak than I have portrayed. But one of the most powerful things about my dad's life is his simplicity. It is not inordinately complex to be a good and loving father. If you look back, most of the chapter titles are brief and simple. Worlds of difference can be made in your family today by slowing down, being an encourager, and making a conscious choice to honor the Lord and prioritize your family. Outside of a growing relationship with Jesus Christ, there is nothing more important in the entire world than building an intimate relationship with your wife and strong relationships with your children. It may take some time to repair the pattern of hurt and neglect, but with God's grace and power I fully believe you can make a great amount of progress in a short time.

Men, you may not have had a father to bless, guide, and encourage you. But in God's strength, you can be the beginning point of something dynamic and life-changing in your family. Give Christ the undisputed first place in your heart.

Make your wife feel that she is the most special person to you on the face of the earth other than the Lord. Encourage her. Live out an example before your children. Put energy into building a relationship with your children. Listen to your children. Talk to your kids about hard stuff. Bless them with your words. Trust God with all you have.

Do all things for the glory of God!

Printed in the United States
219709BV00002B/6/P

9 781615 070336